AF371309

Dike Blair

Dike Blair   Matinee

Edward Hopper House
Museum & Study Center

Dike Blair

in conversation

with

Helen Molesworth

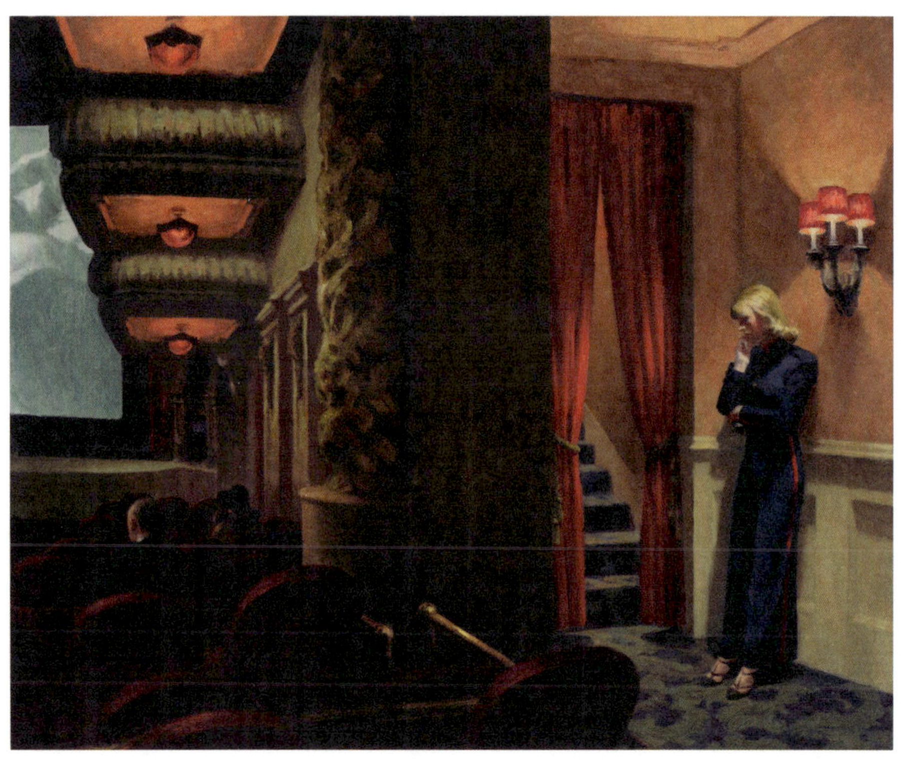

Edward Hopper, *New York Movie*, 1939. Oil on canvas,
32¼ x 40⅛ in. (81.9 x 101.9 cm). Museum of Modern Art, New York

Helen Molesworth: Did I press record? Oh my God.

Dike Blair: Did we lose it all?

HM: I think we did. I'm such a numbskull. [*laughing*] Well, we are at the Museum of Modern Art, New York, to look at Edward Hopper's *New York Movie* (1939), and in preparation for this conversation we both read Brian O'Doherty's 2004 essay "Hopper's Look."[1] Hopper was born in the 1880s, so the idea that O'Doherty knew him personally felt kind of bizarre to me.

DB: To me, too.

HM: It signals the weird way people from another time are also part of your time. For instance, Hopper didn't see a movie with sound until he was forty-five years old, and yet he was making pictures with all this contemporary resonance. O'Doherty recounts his conversations with Hopper as follows: "When I asked a question about what he was after in *Sun in an Empty Room* (1963), he was silent and, on further interrogation, responded emphatically and with some exasperation, 'I'm after ME!'"[2] I wondered if you think about your practice as being a kind of self-portraiture? Is there a "me" you're after?

DB: I think very much so. I've rarely had trouble deciding what I should paint, but I remember having students who couldn't choose a subject. I'm always like, "Well, just reach out your hand. Whatever's within three feet of you is something that is of interest to you. Paint it."

HM: Is the self-portraiture element the part that interests you? Is that where the self is being imaged?

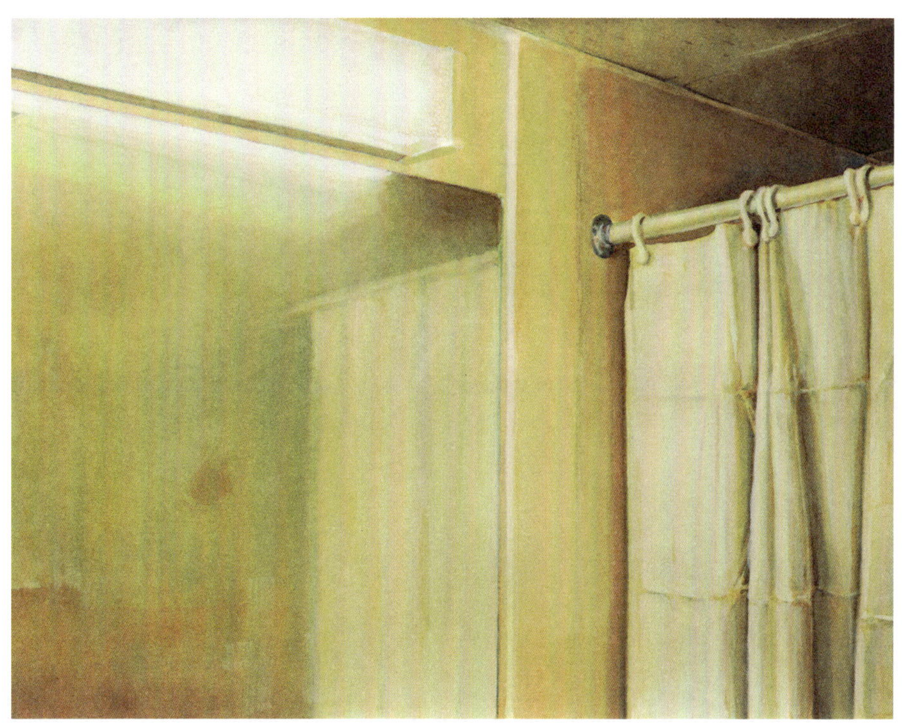

Dike Blair, *Untitled*, 2002. Gouache on paper, 18 × 24 in. (45.7 × 61 cm)

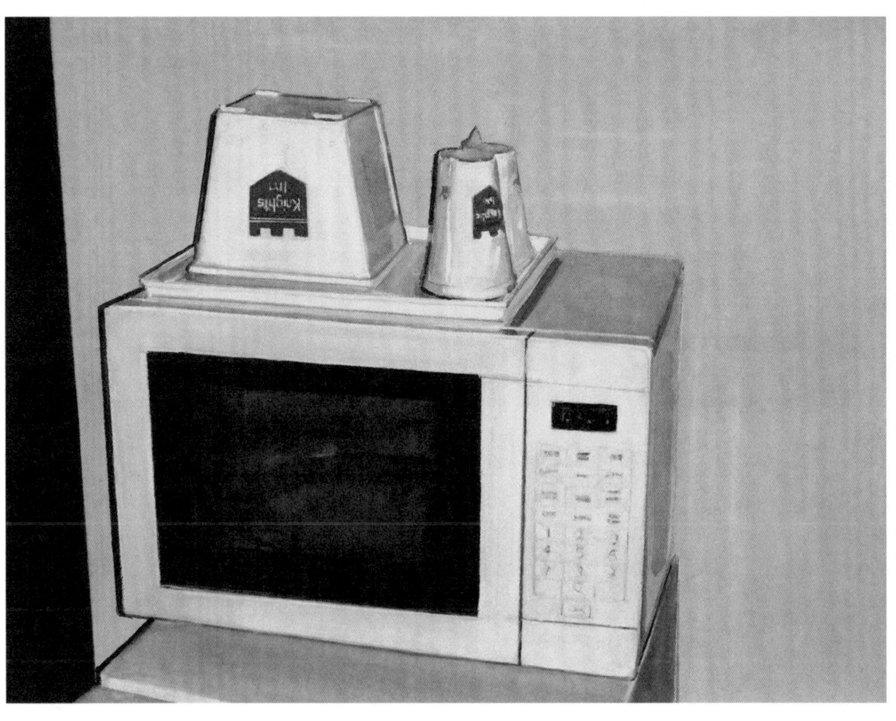

Dike Blair, *Untitled*, 2007. Gouache and pencil on paper, 15 × 20 in. (38.1 × 50.8 cm)

DB: I enjoy the act of painting and I enjoy rendering. I enjoy making a painting that slows someone down more than a photograph can. I like people to enjoy it and enter it. For the most part, my paintings are about pleasure and beauty. That's the kind of art Marie [Abma] and I tend to hang in our house, stuff that brings us both pleasure. On the other hand, there's austerity and that gets us back to Hopper. When I look at his work I don't see, or think, of loneliness. It's the beauty of solitude, and solitude is a pleasure. These are not social situations. My work removes the figure but there's still the person who has looked and taken the time to render what they saw, and so they're all flavored with solitude and self-portraiture.

HM: O'Doherty says Hopper paints transient spaces, interiors where you don't stay for long: hotels, railway carriages . . .

DB: Theaters.

HM: . . . restaurants, diners. Your work shares this quality. I think the first piece of yours that broke my heart was a set of empty seats in an airplane lounge. I thought, *God dammit. That's exactly it*, these spaces produce a kind of ennui and solitude, not quite lonely . . .

DB: There's a real pleasure to it, I think. When you arrive at the airport, there's that . . .

HM: . . . promise of what your aloneness might mean?

DB: I think so. You might sit in a chair and read a book that you wouldn't read in your apartment. Also, when I travel, I take a lot of pictures of things that I'd potentially paint because I'm seeing things fresh. I'm here, I'm looking at this. I don't get to see this every day. When you travel, the act of looking and seeing is amplified.

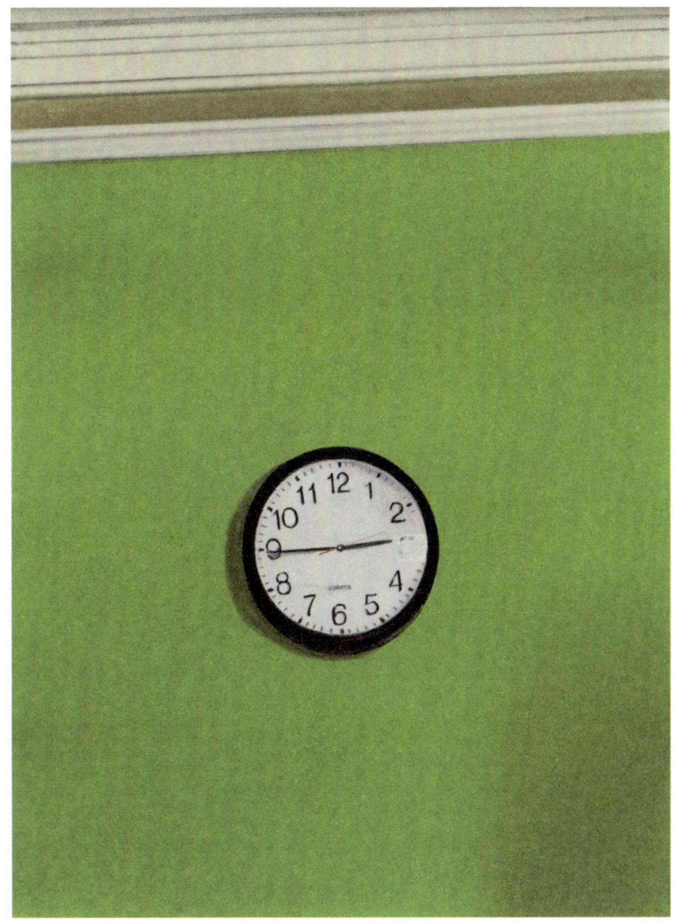

Dike Blair, *Untitled*, 2016. Gouache, pastel, and pencil on paper, 24 × 18 in. (61 × 45.7 cm)

Dike Blair, *Untitled*, 1997. Gouache on paper, 12 × 16 in. (30.5 × 40.6 cm)

HM: When O'Doherty writes of Hopper's spaces that they "all have to do with temporary occupancy," he has the advantage of hindsight.[3] I'm curious if you have a sense that you are building an oeuvre based on the kinds of spaces you make pictures of?

DB: No. When you do artist talks, you create an armature to discuss the work, but I don't carry that into the studio. I look and take pictures. I think I'm more focused on the editorial process. There might be six paintings I'd like to do all at the same time because each would require a different technique. That's my strategy, as opposed to thinking, "What am I building?" Right now, everything I'm doing is right outside our door: I'm painting skies, or the ground with footprints. Most of the images are within fifty yards of where I sleep, which is so much fun.

HM: What makes that fun?

DB: Well, there's an economy to it—a simplicity and a kind of pleasure. For years I'd wanted to paint skies, but in New York you're looking at buildings, not skies, and then our old place was covered by woods. Now, we're on top of a hill, and I see skies all day. Each day is different. They're gorgeous.

HM: I have that when we are in Provincetown. I feel like I'm high on the sky all the time. I'm constantly saying to my wife, "Oh, you have to come outside and look at this." At some point she said, "You know this happens every day, right?" [*laughing*] I just couldn't believe how good it made me feel, how expansive and how marvelous.

DB: When you were sixteen, or even twenty-five—would you have had anywhere near that kind of experience?

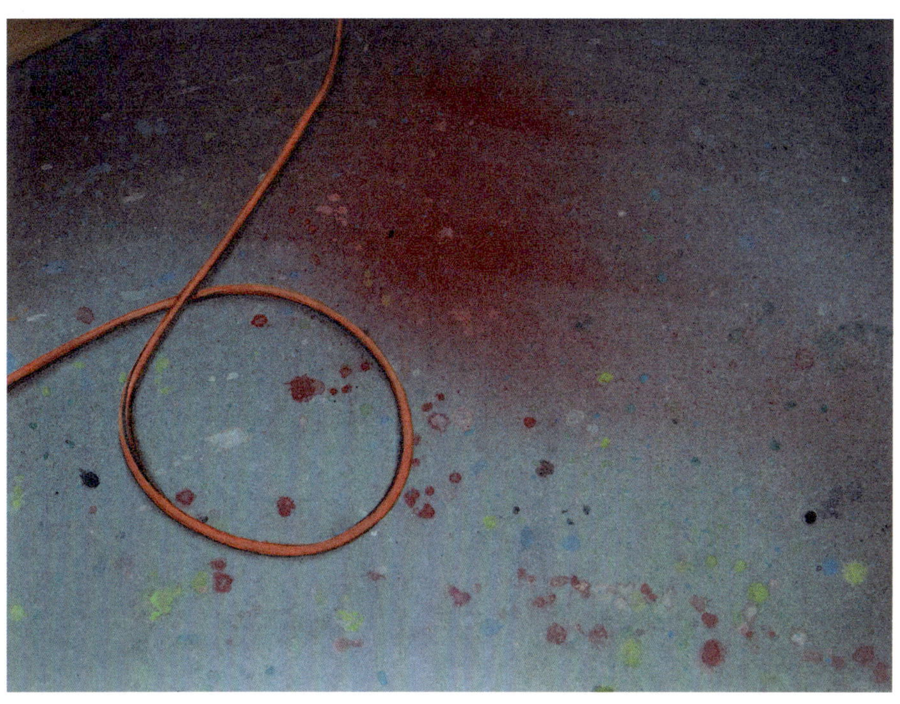

Dike Blair, *Untitled*, 2013. Gouache and pastel on paper, 15 × 20 in. (38.1 × 50.8 cm)

HM: I think I might have. I was always very sensitive to light. I always had a sense that light was a palpable thing, that it wasn't neutral. Maybe that's why I love painting.

DB: When it comes to Hopper, a lot of people talk about architecture. For me, the light is more important. But I really didn't think too deeply about Hopper until art historian Robert Hobbs visited my studio and proposed doing an exhibition juxtaposing our works. That was certainly an exhilarating prospect, and I started studying Hopper very seriously.

HM: When we first sat down in front of *New York Movie*, you said that as a painter, you look first at the light. You talked about how you paint from light to dark because you can darken things more easily than you can lighten them. When you look at this work, at what point do you stop looking at *how* he's painted it to see *what* he has painted? I don't know how he's painted it, so for me it is always and forever an image. But for you, it's both process and image.

DB: Of course, we all look at paintings differently. Sometimes if I go to a show with an art historian and they know an awful lot about Napoleon's history . . . well, I don't know much about Napoleon and I don't care much about him. What I like is the way the light might be coming off his hat or something. The whole time we've been sitting here I've been thinking about this spiral column, the stairway down, and the slope back up. The construction of this painting shows the architecture of movie theaters of that era but, more importantly, creates a pictorial space that's wonderfully spiraled.

HM: Why do you think it's important for him to show the stairs?

DB: I think it makes the space more interesting and complex.

HM: I feel like both the stairs and the screen are offering entrance and egress to another world.

DB: Yeah, there are multiple worlds in this one painting. Hobbs made the observation that Hopper relies on the "missing parts of a narrative."[4] He also writes that if the "assumed observer of this painting . . . were entering the theater, the usherette would no doubt take notice."[5] I was pondering that, and I'm not sure that Hopper creates a viewer with that much presence, but Hobbs is absolutely correct that our eyes navigate the architecture of the painting much like a person would.

HM: I don't know if the viewer is in the picture.

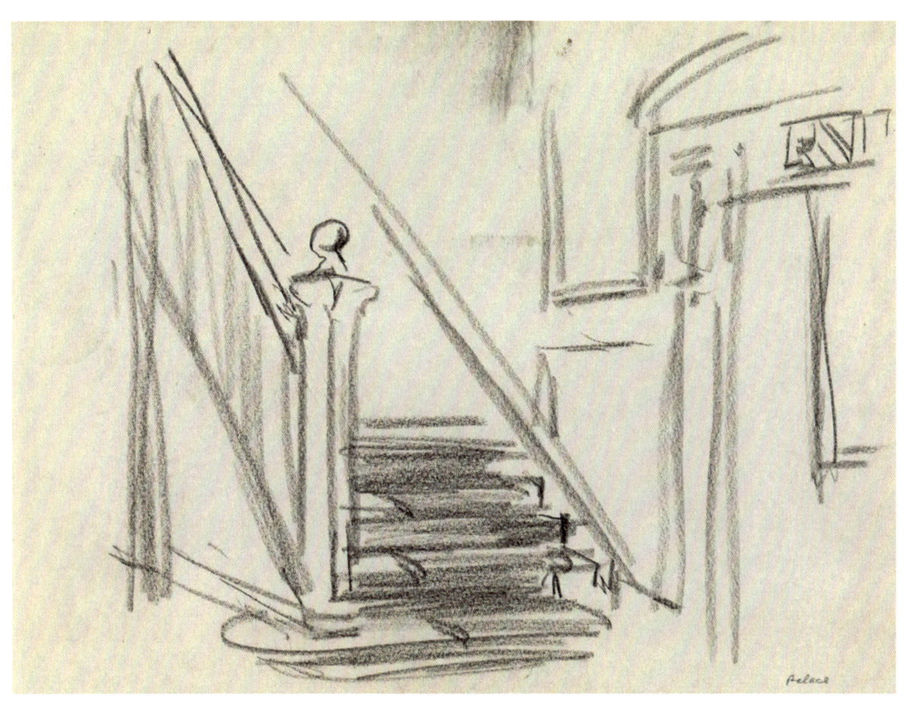

Edward Hopper, *Study for New York Movie (Palace theatre)*, 1938.
Fabricated chalk on paper, 8⅞ × 11⅞ in. (22.5 × 30.2 cm). Whitney Museum
of American Art, New York; Josephine N. Hopper Bequest

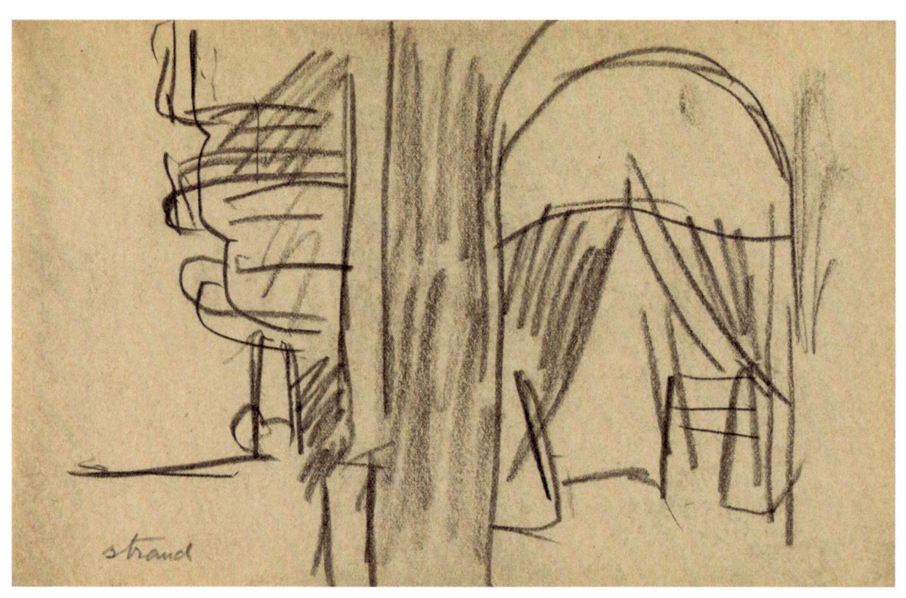

Edward Hopper, *Study for New York Movie (Strand theatre)*, 1938.
Fabricated chalk on paper, 4½ × 7¼ in. (11.3 × 18.4 cm). Whitney Museum
of American Art, New York; Josephine N. Hopper Bequest

DB: Exactly. Or, since we're also talking about O'Doherty, perhaps that imagined viewer is his *eye*, not his *spectator*.

HM: You pointed out this spiral column, but I'm obsessed with this flat piece of architecture or wall right next to it. For me this nearly blank wall is functioning like the tree in the John Baldessari painting about how not to make a picture [*Wrong*, 1966–68]—the one where a tree comes right out of his head, pretty much smack dab in the middle of the canvas.

DB: I'd never even given that a thought, but you're completely right. I mean, in the Hopper painting, it's this dull, massive thing. And yet it doesn't disturb the flow. I mean, it completely makes you flow in other directions, in a spiral.

HM: When you are looking at the process of a painting, do you ever look at the light from the sconces falling on the usherette and think, "I'm going to steal that," or is there a way that the paint is applied, or the space has been articulated, that you are filing away to use later?

DB: I've certainly painted images with that kind of direct, cast light. Here, that faint reflection on the brass rail excites me more. It's so subtle, yet so necessary—it allows the eye to move over the monolith we were discussing above and follow the stairs up to the right.

HM: Is part of the pleasure of looking at a painting for you knowing how it's made? I'm a pretty good home cook, so when I'm in a restaurant eating really elevated food, I'm asking myself, "How'd they make this?" And when I can't figure it out, I'm super interested. Is there something you can't figure out in this?

DB: No. What awes me is that I would never attempt a painting this complicated or big or time-consuming. I can see him piecing

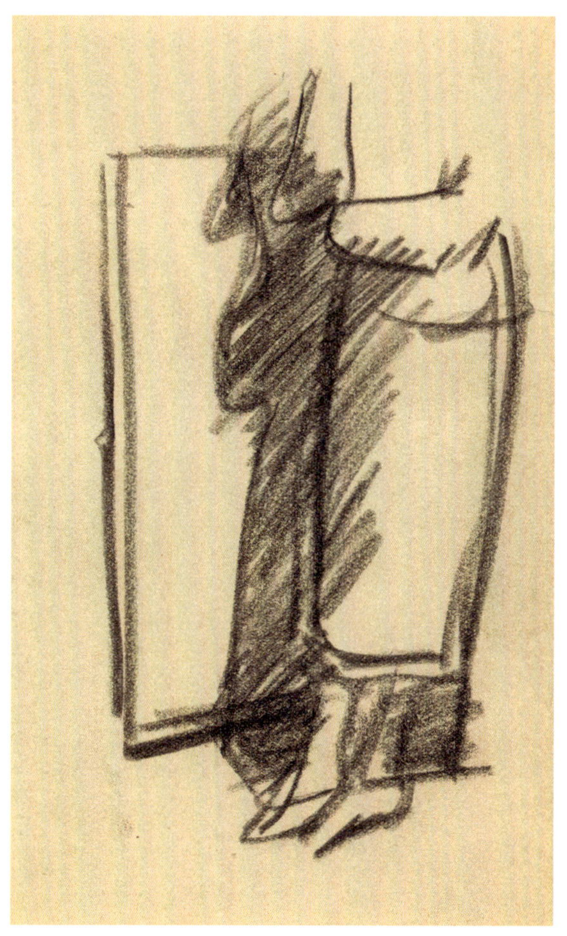

Edward Hopper, *Study for New York Movie*, 1938. Fabricated chalk on paper, 7¼ × 4½ in. (18.4 × 11.3 cm). Whitney Museum of American Art, New York; Josephine N. Hopper Bequest

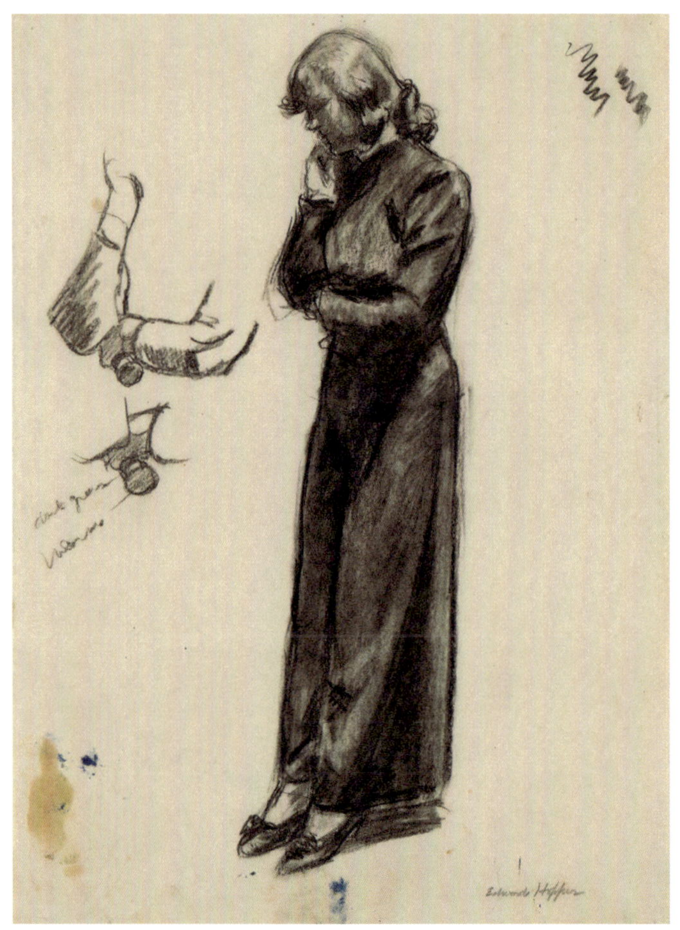

Edward Hopper, *Study for New York Movie*, 1939. Fabricated chalk
and charcoal on paper, 15 × 11⅛ in. (37.9 × 28.3cm). Whitney Museum
of American Art, New York; Josephine N. Hopper Bequest

together all the drawings, the architecture, the drawings of Jo [Hopper]. I think he had to do multiple sessions with her because then he decided, "Oh yeah, I want you to hold the flashlight." Composing and working at this scale is a six-month commitment.

HM: That's amazing. Why don't you? Is it about scale or time—and we know space and time are inextricable.

DB: Exactly. Whenever I've attempted it, if I want to bring the level of finish that I tend to bring things, it's too tedious. I don't have assistants to do all the underpainting—that's just not how I work—and neither did Hopper. I know how he does it, but I couldn't do it, psychologically. In truth, I'm too impatient and I like the modesty of my scale.

HM: There's a sense in your imagery of something having just happened or something about to happen. The Hopper literature is full of people projecting an enormous amount of narrative onto his paintings, even though I feel like he's working awfully hard to not have that happen. I don't know if you are also trying hard to not have that happen. I would argue that Hopper's compositions say, "I'm here to show you something that I've framed for you rather than to tell you a story." I don't know why people want to make up a big story about Hopper, why they can't handle his work's liminality.

DB: I agree with you, but we are probably in the minority. Lawrence Block edited *In Sunlight or in Shadow*, a book of short fiction inspired by Hopper by some great writers. To my mind they were interesting, but none seem to *get* the Hopper that I see. Liminality is one thing I think about in the studio. Because I paint skies and windows and I think of painting itself as being liminal space.

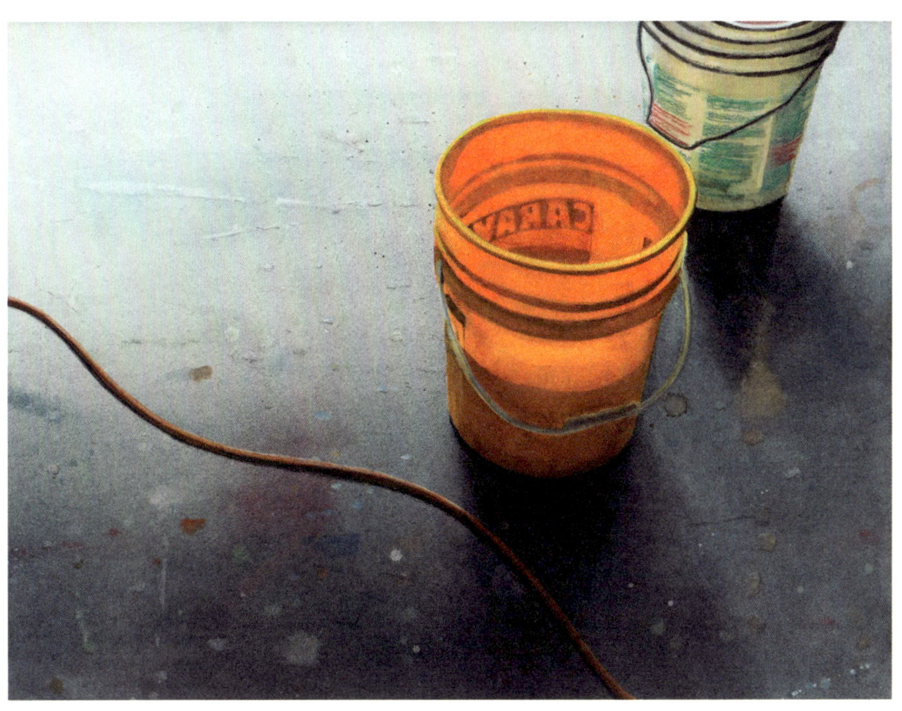

Dike Blair, *Untitled*, 2015. Gouache on paper, 18 × 24 in. (45.7 × 61 cm)

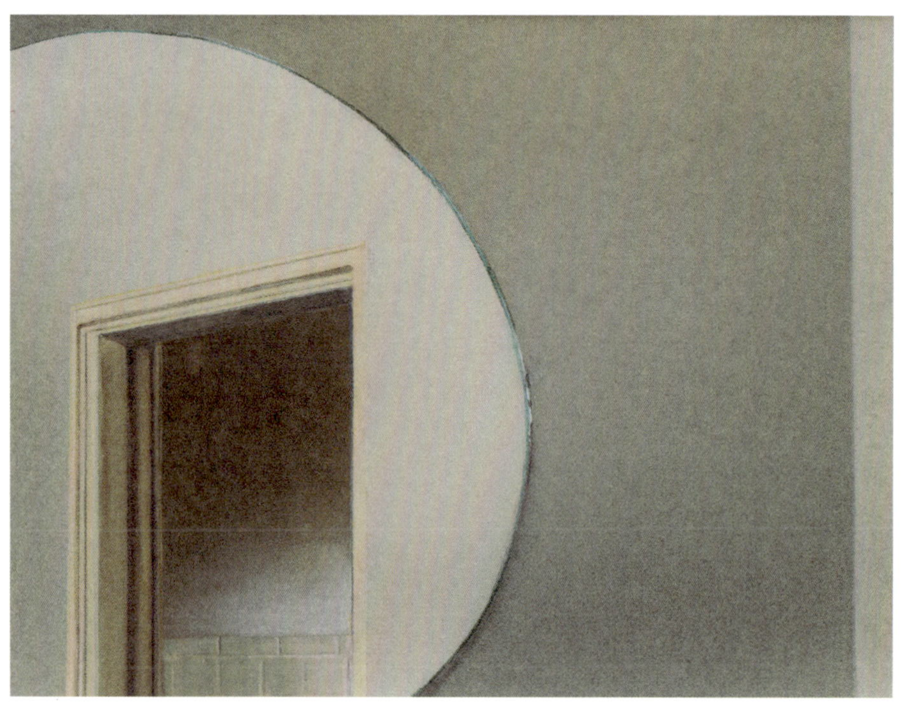

Dike Blair, *Untitled*, 2016. Gouache, pastel, and pencil on paper,
15 × 20 in. (38.1 × 50.8 cm)

HM: How so?

DB: Well, a painter creates an illusionistic space on a two-dimensional surface, a picture plane. When we enter or pass through that plane, we cooperate with the illusion. I think this even happens—perhaps in a more metaphysical way—with non-objective art. It does seem that people have a really hard time resisting the urge to apply narrative to everything, even when an artist tells us not to. That denial of narrative becomes a narrative in itself.

HM: Cinematic space also pretends to be real but isn't, just like how painterly space is not real, but two-dimensional. When you said, "I like to render," are you working to make your own painterly space believable? O'Doherty defines realism as "a depicted universe that is imaginatively continuous with our own, where the physics of things and their perception behave synonymously with what we see every day and can be so tested."[6] Do you jive with that?

DB: Yeah, I do. I had to read that sentence a couple of times to unpack it. I think the painter's depicted universe needs to establish and follow rules somewhat consistently; it should have an internal logic, as we like to imagine our universe does. There are wonderful moments of synesthesia when painting, perhaps Hopper had one when he was painting the usherette's hair? Or I might have one when I get a coffee mug handle just right. For me, those moments are the result of when, in the act of representation, I feel an utter connection with the represented.

HM: That's the sweet spot.

DB: It's really special. I think Hopper probably had a blast painting that movie screen . . .

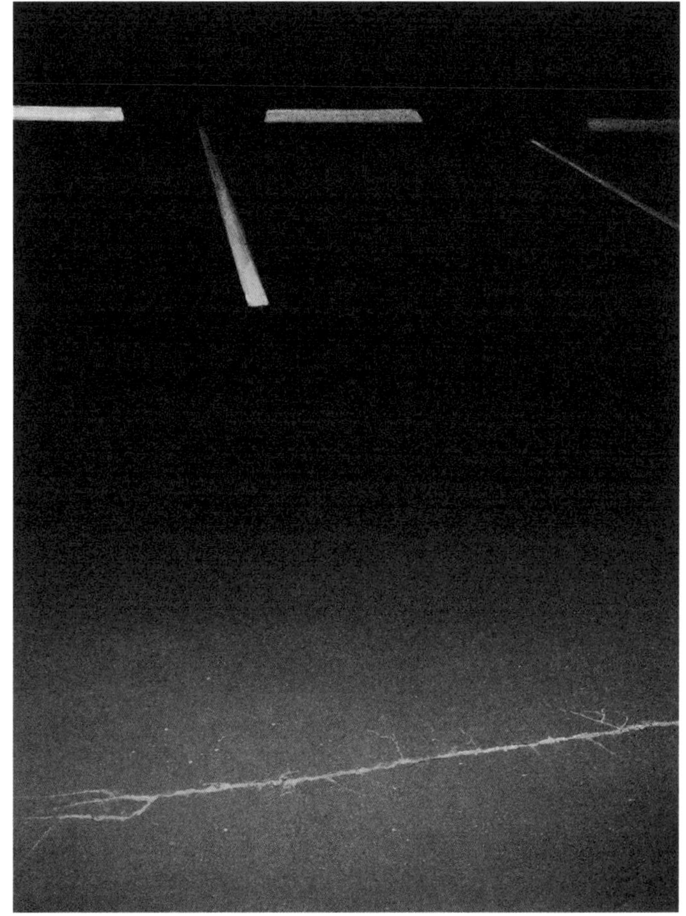

Dike Blair, *Untitled*, 2009. Gouache on paper, 20 × 15 in. (50.8 × 38.1 cm)

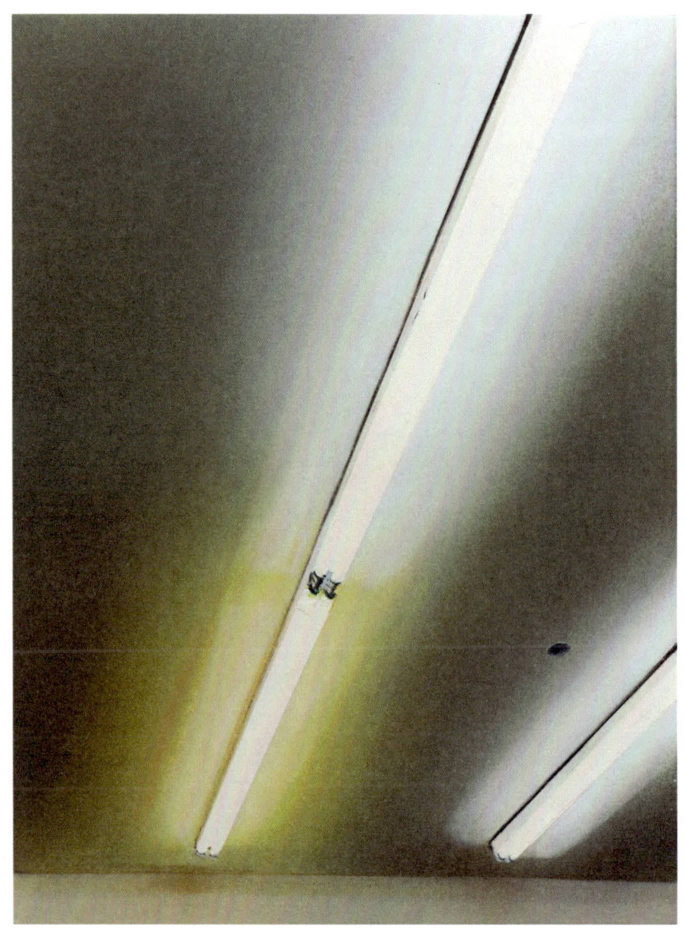

Dike Blair, *Untitled*, 2020. Oil on aluminum, 28 × 21 in. (71.1 × 53.3 cm)

HM: It's so abstract, that movie screen. There are these moments when Hopper was known as the great realist of his era. And yet in the century of abstraction, there are so many passages here.

DB: The screen is lit with cool, projected light, and also with a very faint, warm, ambient light at the bottom. One might not even see nor think to capture that effect.

HM: How did you, generationally speaking, give yourself the permission to engage in beauty? It was not a word that people used in the 1970s, '80s, and '90s.

DB: I think during the '80s I began to accept that the subjects I was attracted to might have been dismissed as being "pretty." By the '90s, talk of beauty became more permissible because of Dave Hickey, and I was a fan. I've tried to avoid being too romantic or sentimental, although not always successfully. One thing I always try to keep in mind is to really consider doing things that my brain says "no" to.

HM: So you're contrary with yourself?

DB: I think paying attention to reflexive self-censorship can reveal something interesting.

HM: The other thing O'Doherty wrote about Hopper that made me think about your work was that "he dispensed completely with irony, or at least with the scathing variety through which modernism tested established conventions."[7] Your pictures are not ironic, are they? *You* are ironic sometimes . . .

DB: Yes, and I've said that I don't think anyone—or nearly anyone—in my generation can do anything without some element of irony. When I first started painting my gouaches,

I was depicting scenes like sailboats on the water, or a highway at night. At the time, painting those subjects had a mild irony to me. Perhaps the aforementioned self-censorship had something to do with that. When the voice in my head says I shouldn't paint some subject, very often I do.

HM: How about painting a martini glass and a cocktail napkin on a bar?

DB: Again, there's a little bit of the irony of, "Who's this guy painting this martini? Why is it so beautiful and compelling?" And I started painting cocktails when I quit drinking—which lasted eight years. At this point in time, at my age and this stage of my career, it's all established, I don't know . . .

HM: Wait, are you saying that at a certain point you don't need irony anymore? Do we age out of it?

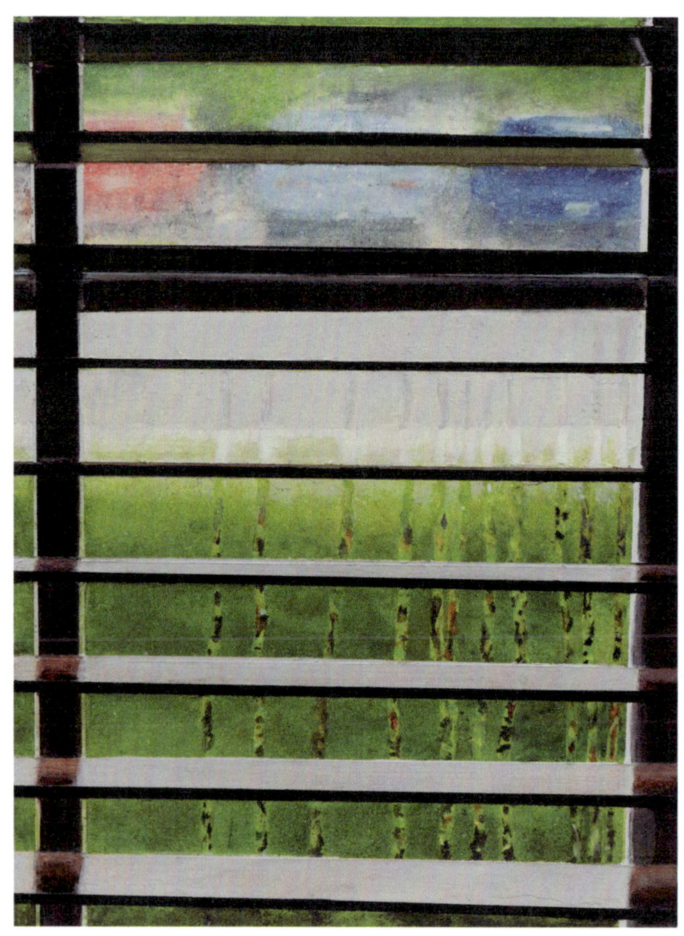

Dike Blair, *Untitled*, 2022. Oil on aluminum, 16 × 12 in. (40.6 × 30.5 cm)

DB: Well, I think we might. You're a generation or two down from me. I'm more Richard Prince's generation, and he and I are friends and I think about his work a lot. Richard will make an image of the Marlboro Man and it's thick with cultural commentary and irony. I'll paint a pack of Marlboros that I smoked and really enjoyed, and I loved the way the light hit it. I feel these works might be related, except that mine is maybe romantic, maybe even a little sentimental, and his is ruthless and ironic.

HM: Do you think that O'Doherty is right, that Hopper has no irony?

DB: I studied his watercolors when I was working on the *Gloucester* show, and I can say that there's no irony there.[8] That's very dry stuff, although Hobbs, who curated the show, suggests they possess some class-related invective. As far as Hopper's later works, like the motels, I'm not so sure. O'Doherty remembers that Hopper "accepted things as they were, whether he approved of them or not. He did not think matters were subject to much improvement."[9] Perhaps that gimlet-eye worldview flavors his work with a little irony.

HM: I wonder if that *"plus ça change"* attitude is why his work always feels so current—do you know what I mean? We are looking at a painting of a kind of space that doesn't exist anymore (a large, proscenium movie theater with a red-velvet curtain), and "usherette" is a role that doesn't exist anymore, so we could see this painting as hopelessly about the past—

DB: I'm not sure exactly why the paintings don't seem dated. You noted how interesting it was that O'Doherty, someone I think of as very contemporary, felt contemporary with and was in conversation with Hopper about his work. I think it's also related to something

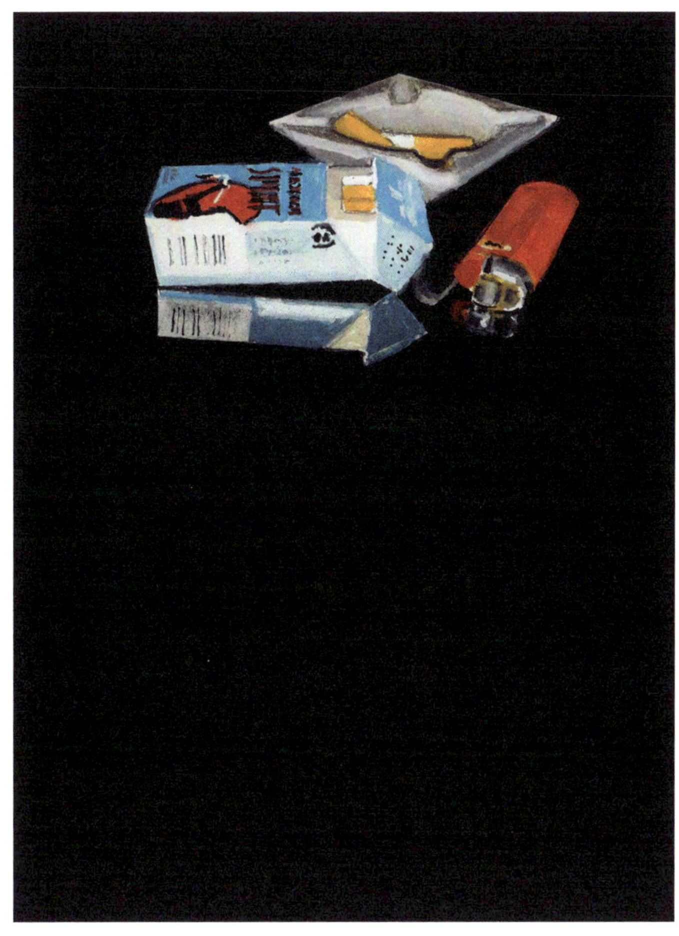

Dike Blair, *Untitled*, 2017. Gouache and pencil on paper, 10 × 7½ in. (25.4 × 19 cm)

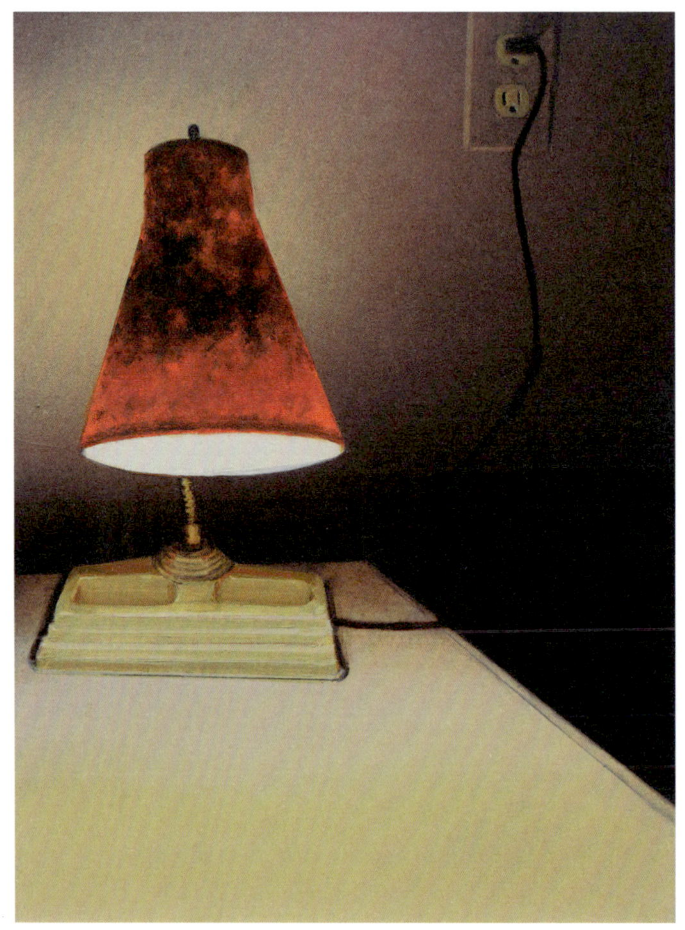

Dike Blair, *Untitled*, 2021. Oil on aluminum, 16 × 12 in. (40.6 × 30.5 cm)

you said earlier, about Hopper giving us something he framed, rather than telling a story.

HM: How do you read the usherette? I mean it's obviously a deliberate choice that we don't see anyone actively seeing the movie.

DB: Well, I thought that the seated man and woman were a couple, but you correctly noted that they were sitting apart. It's so much better that they're sitting apart in a darkened space and that we don't see their eyes. We also studied the usherette's eyes and decided that they weren't closed but that she's looking downward—we have the impression she's in a world inside her head that's apart from the theater's world. I find her so much more compelling than any of Hopper's other women.

HM: It's funny how even in a painting as "straight" as this one we still must parse *some* kind of narrative—are they a couple, does the usherette watch the film or not? O'Doherty says: "The paintings are presented with a neutrality that has invited contradictory readings."[10] There's something like neutrality in your work, too. We're offered this space that is constructed with a degree of concentration that, as a result, means we completely believe in this space.

DB: Are we talking about me or Hopper?

HM: Both. You both create painted space that we as the viewer believe. I wonder, do you think about neutrality when you make your space? Do you think neutrality is a way for the pictures to avoid looking dated? Do we get contradiction because it's neutral?

DB: Well, I was talking about this last night with a friend. I was showing him some images I was thinking about painting. One was a picture taken in an airport bar showing a black-and-white Fellini film on one

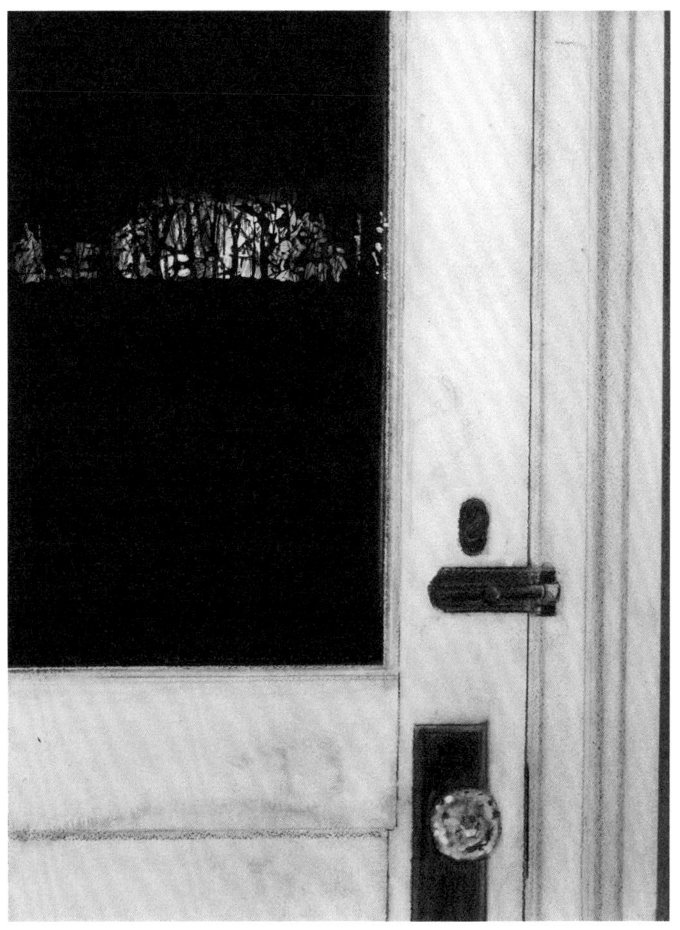

Dike Blair, *Untitled*, 2021. Charcoal, oil, gouache, and gesso on paper,
20⅛ × 15⅛ in. (50.8 × 38.1 cm)

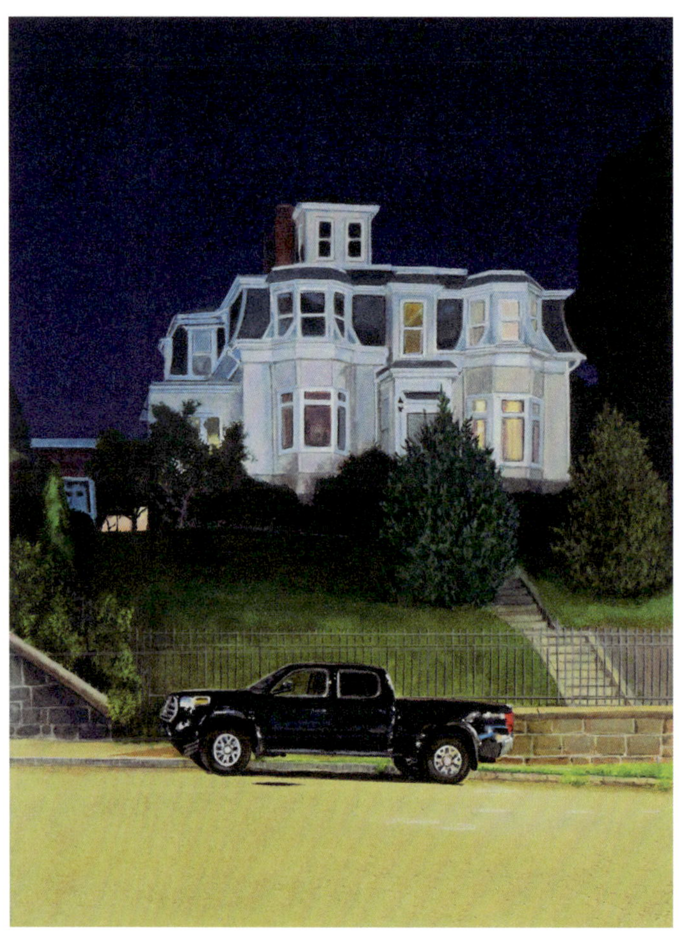

Dike Blair, *Untitled (Gloucester)*, 2022. Gouache and pencil on paper,
28 × 21 in. (71.1 × 53.3 cm)

flat-screen, and a SpongeBob cartoon on another. I've been thinking about whether to paint it for a number of months, and I keep saying "no" because it seems like it's not neutral. It generates some kind of judgment.

HM: Because it invites taste? And taste has a time stamp?

DB: That's it. I remember when I was painting these still lifes of VHS boxes, and some audio cassettes, and I was thinking, wow, I'm really on the cutting edge here. It didn't take long for those paintings to feel nostalgic. I usually want my subjects to be both very personal and specific to me, and also common to many of us.

HM: Right. I have one more thing I wanted to ask you. I'm quoting again from the O'Doherty essay. He writes that Hopper "avoided drawing attention to paint and process. The aim was to keep the spectator right there, looking."[11] I wondered, because I am such an image whore, just looking at the picture all the time, do you avoid process?

DB: I have an aversion to gesture, to visible gesture. I'm allowing it more and more as I get older, probably as my control and eyes get worse. I think of [Robert] Rauschenberg's *Factum I* and *Factum II* (both 1957) and him making the same gesture across two works, thus demystifying the its uniqueness. I came up during a period of a lot of gestural painting and I think it's hard to do it and be genuine. There's a lot of *not* genuine gestural painting, so I avoid it.

HM: Right. When you avoid gesture or avoid leaving traces of process, do you have a sense that it engenders, as O'Doherty says, a viewer who just keeps looking, who doesn't get pulled out of the space of looking?

DB: I don't know, sometimes when you're

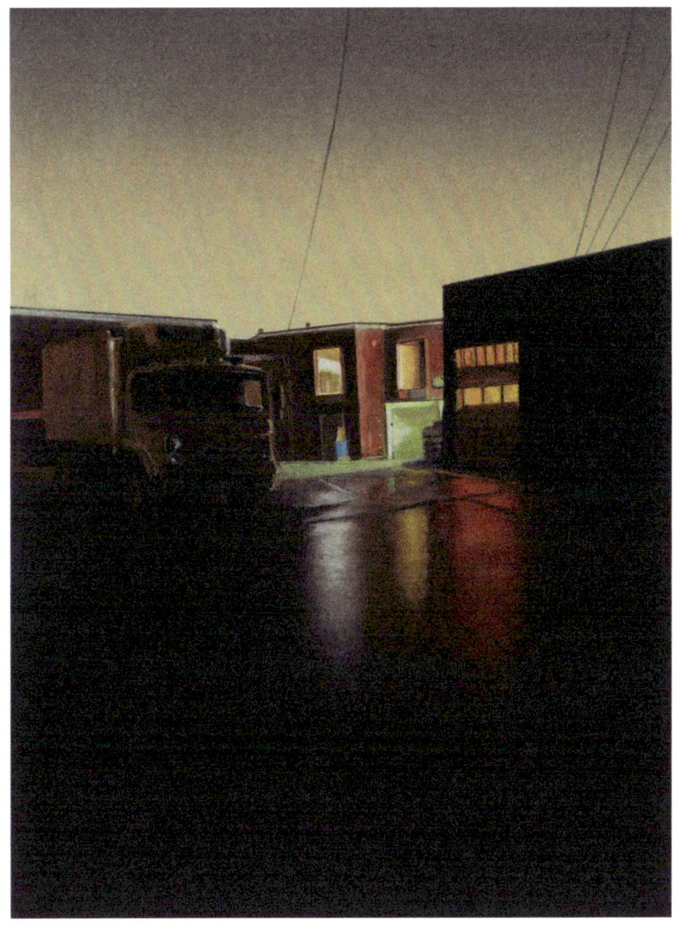

Dike Blair, *Untitled (Gloucester)*, 2021. Gouache and pencil on paper,
24 × 18 in. (61 × 45.7 cm)

looking at a John Singer Sargent and you just see this amazing brushstroke, then maybe you've left the painting for a little bit. But if I could make a gesture like Sargent, I would.

HM: Like the gesture of the light on the rail.

DB: It's still pretty modest. I think it's still puritanical.

HM: Do you think Hopper's giving into something there? Or is that stroke suturing us into the space?

DB: I think it has something to do, too, with that opaque monolith that you mentioned. If you make it opaque all the way down, you're in big trouble.

HM: Right. Well, I'm looking forward to finding that stroke in a painting of yours coming to a movie theater sometime soon.

1. Brian O'Doherty, "Hopper's Look," in *Edward Hopper* (London: Tate, 2004), 82–97.
2. Ibid., 86.
3. Ibid., 92.
4. Robert Hobbs, *Edward Hopper* (New York: Harry N. Abrams, 1987), 20.
5. Ibid., 111.
6. O'Doherty, "Hopper's Look," 83.
7. Ibid., 85.
8. Edward Hopper and Dike Blair, *Gloucester*, Karma, New York, November 10–December 21, 2022.
9. O'Doherty, 85.
10. Ibid., 86.
11. Ibid., 90.

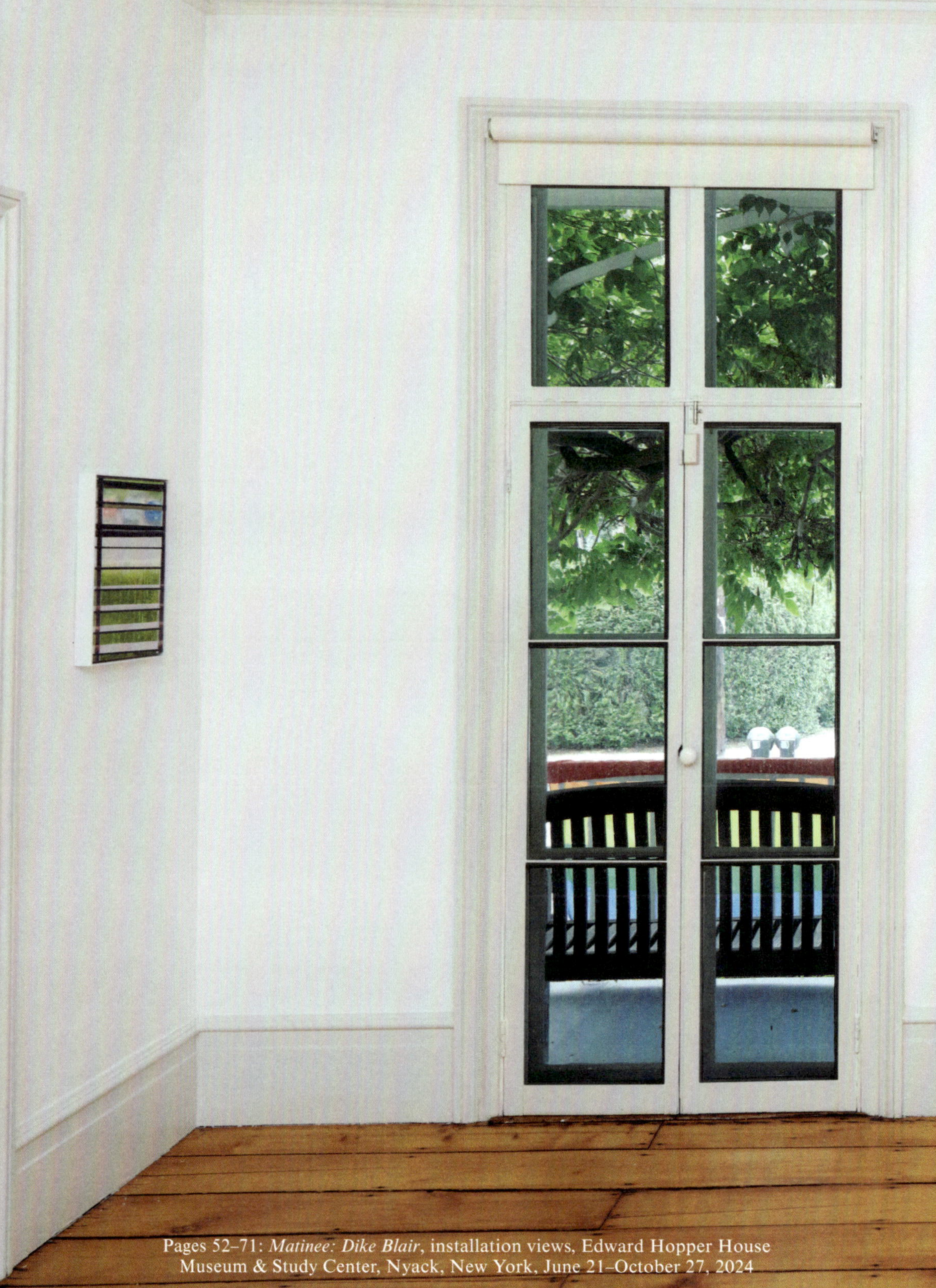

Pages 52–71: *Matinee: Dike Blair*, installation views, Edward Hopper House Museum & Study Center, Nyack, New York, June 21–October 27, 2024

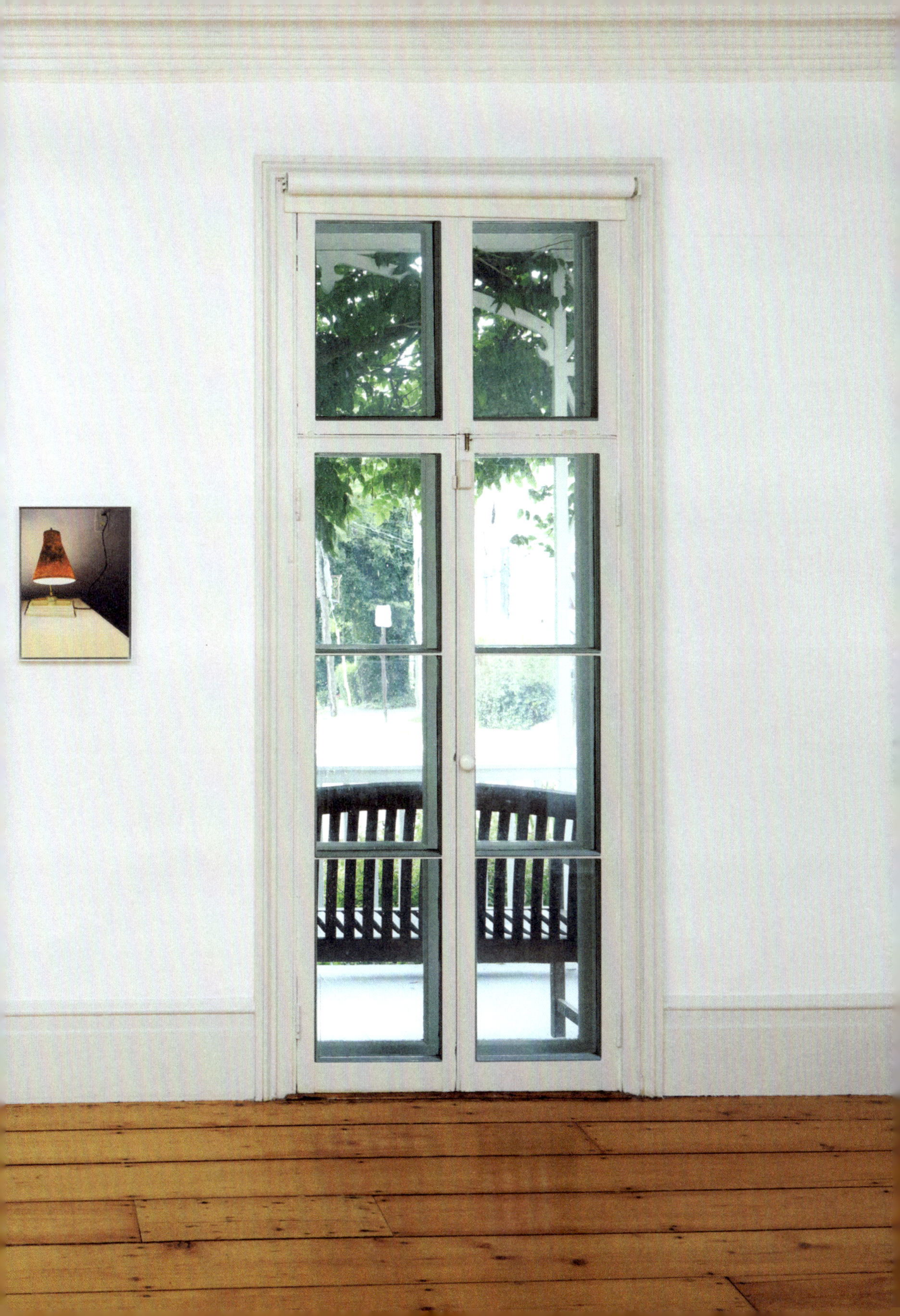

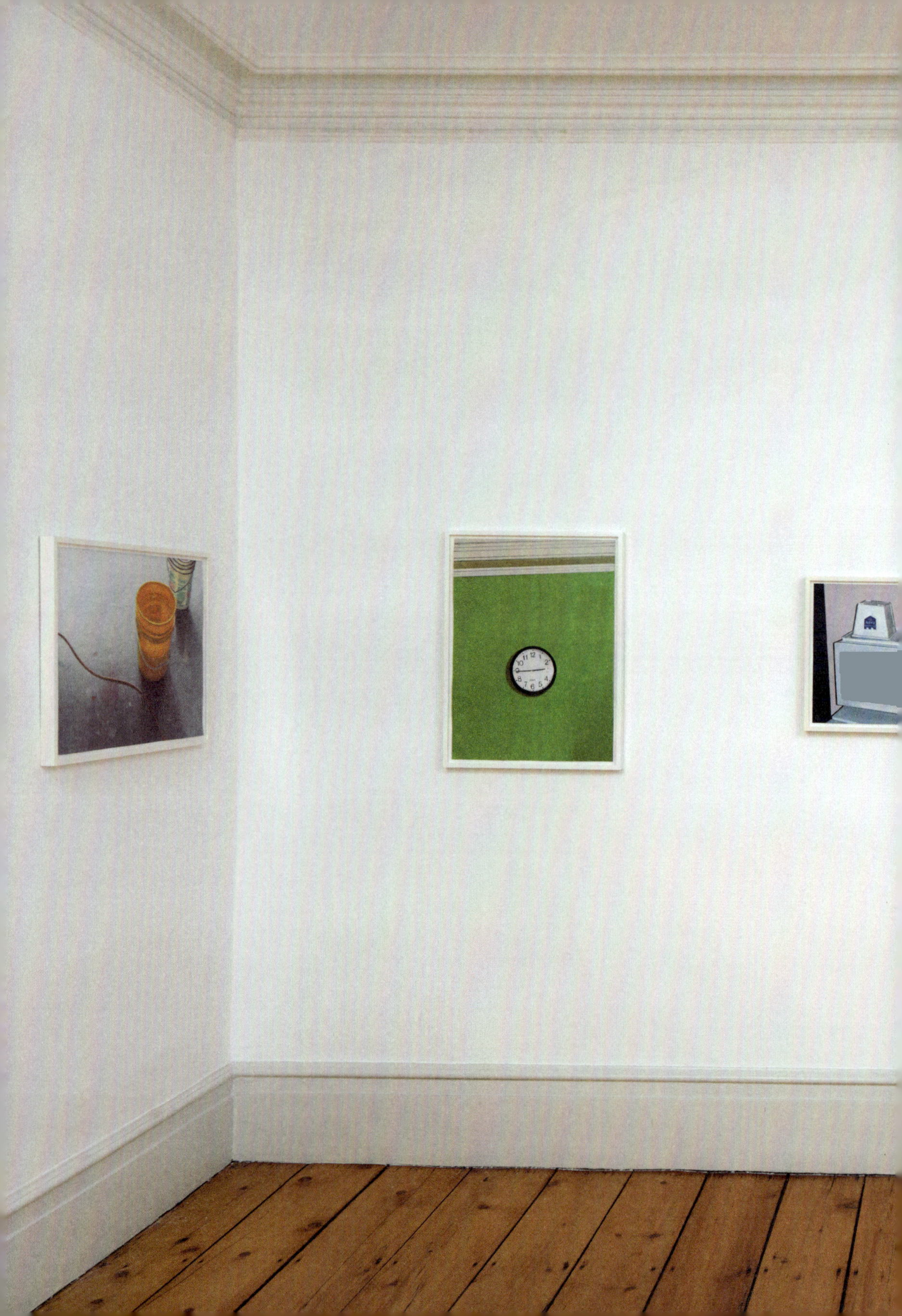

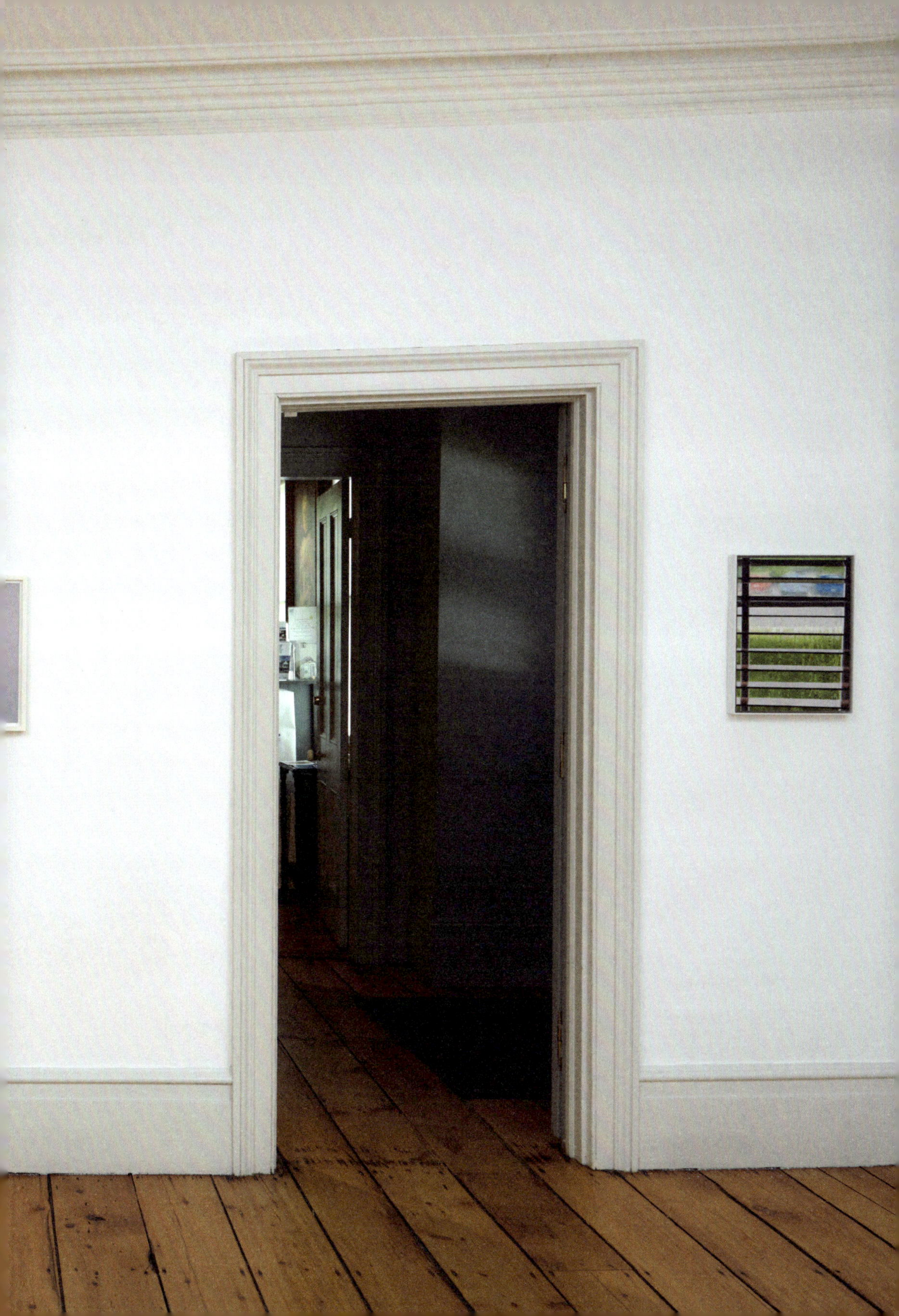

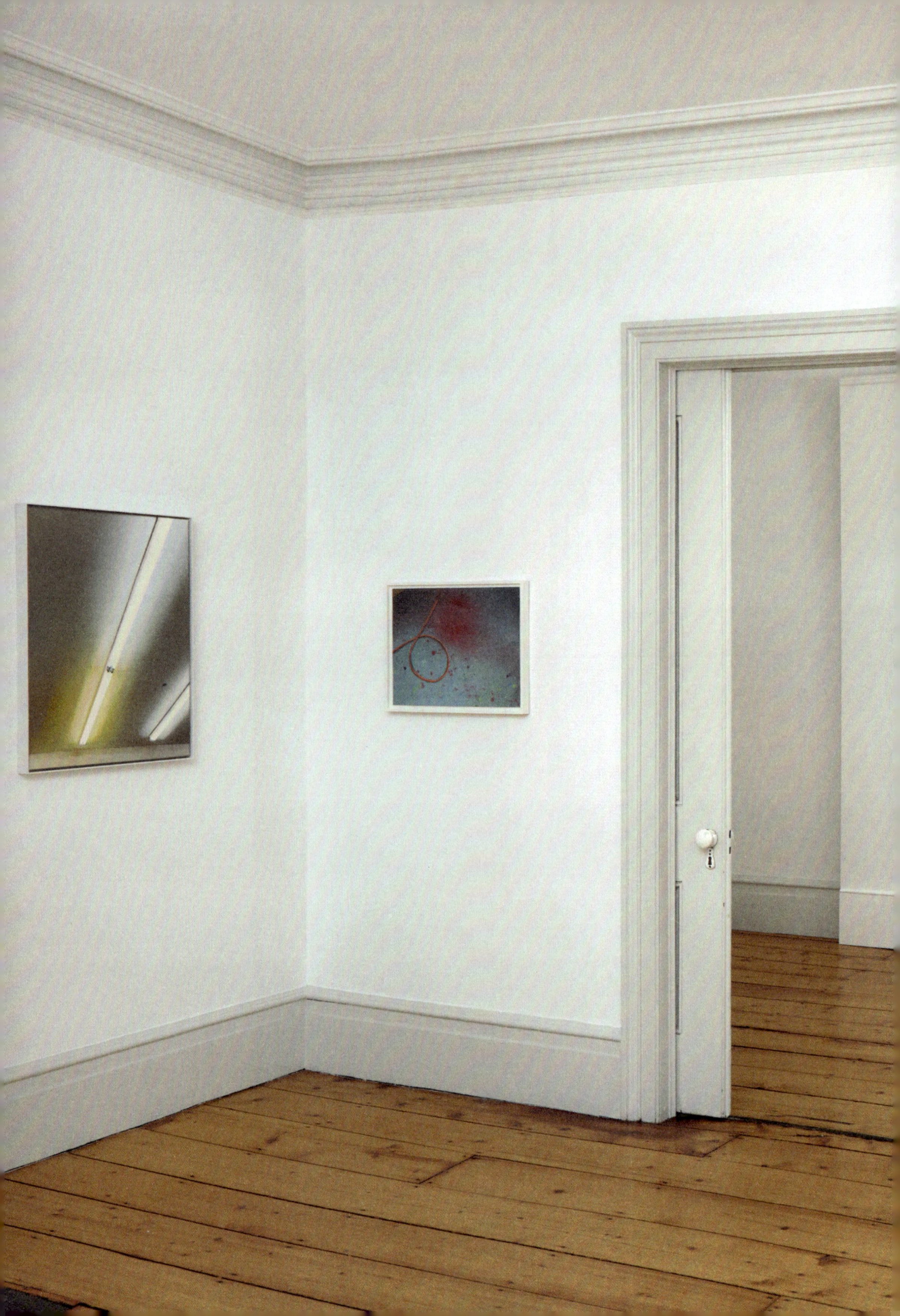

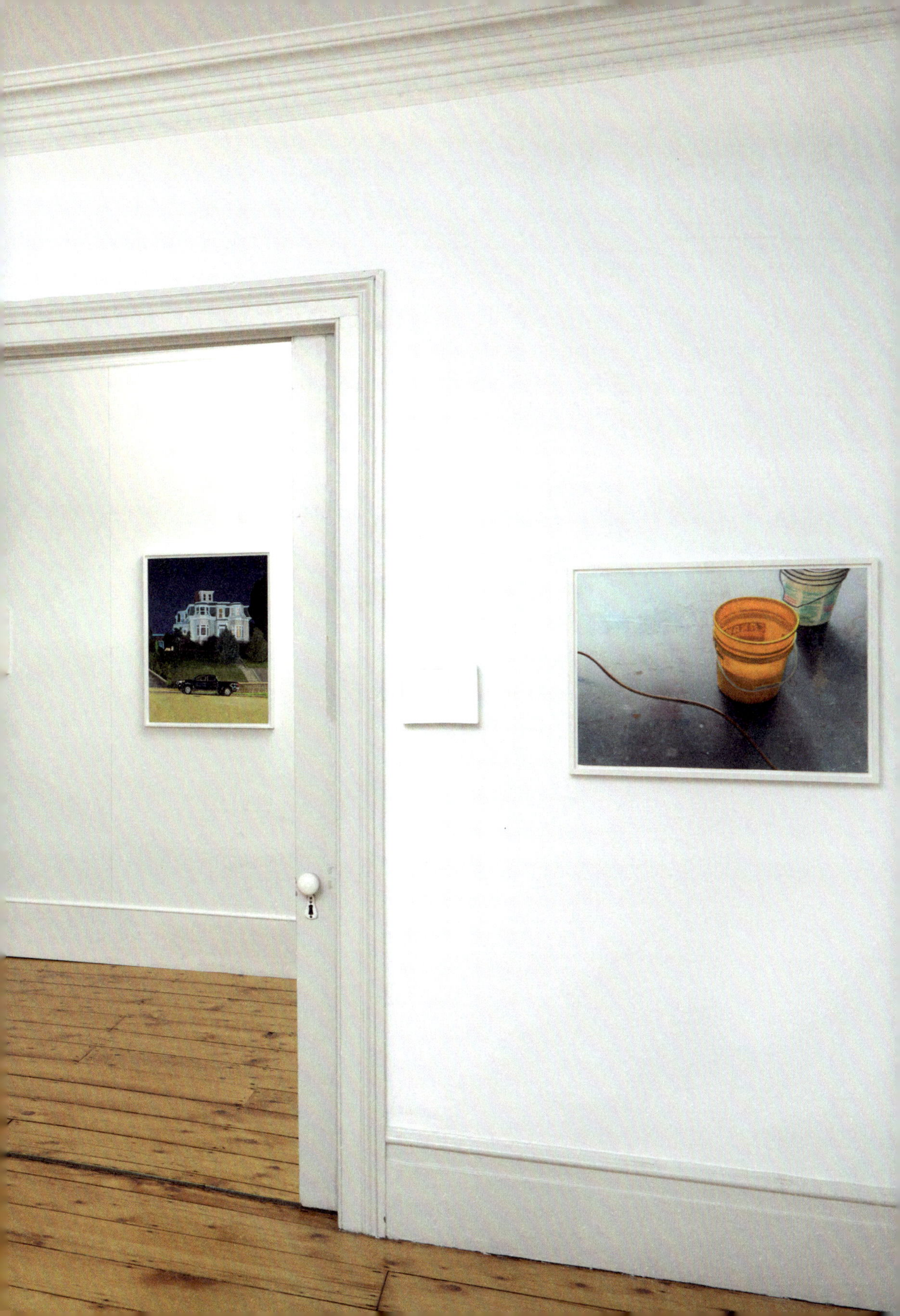

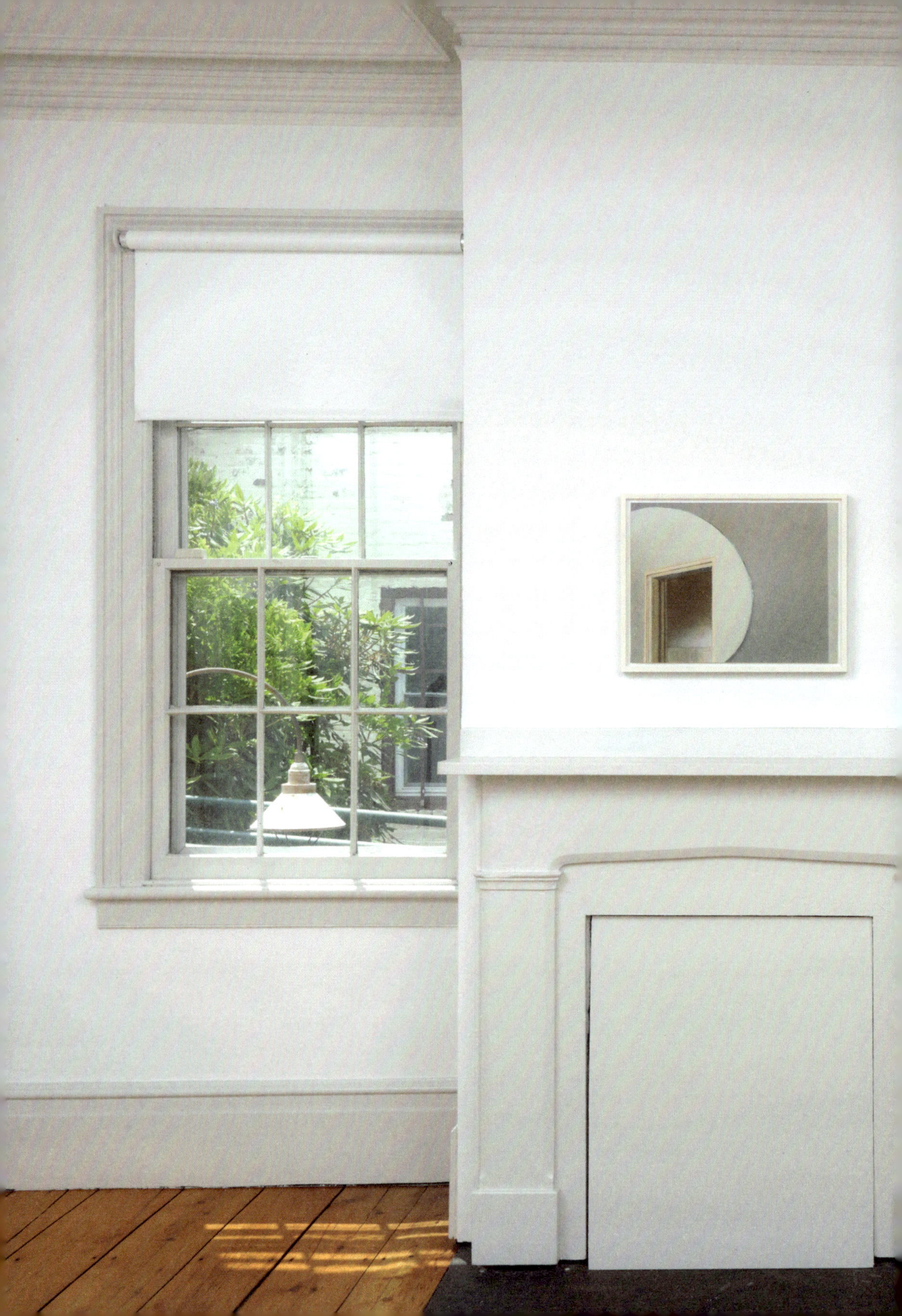

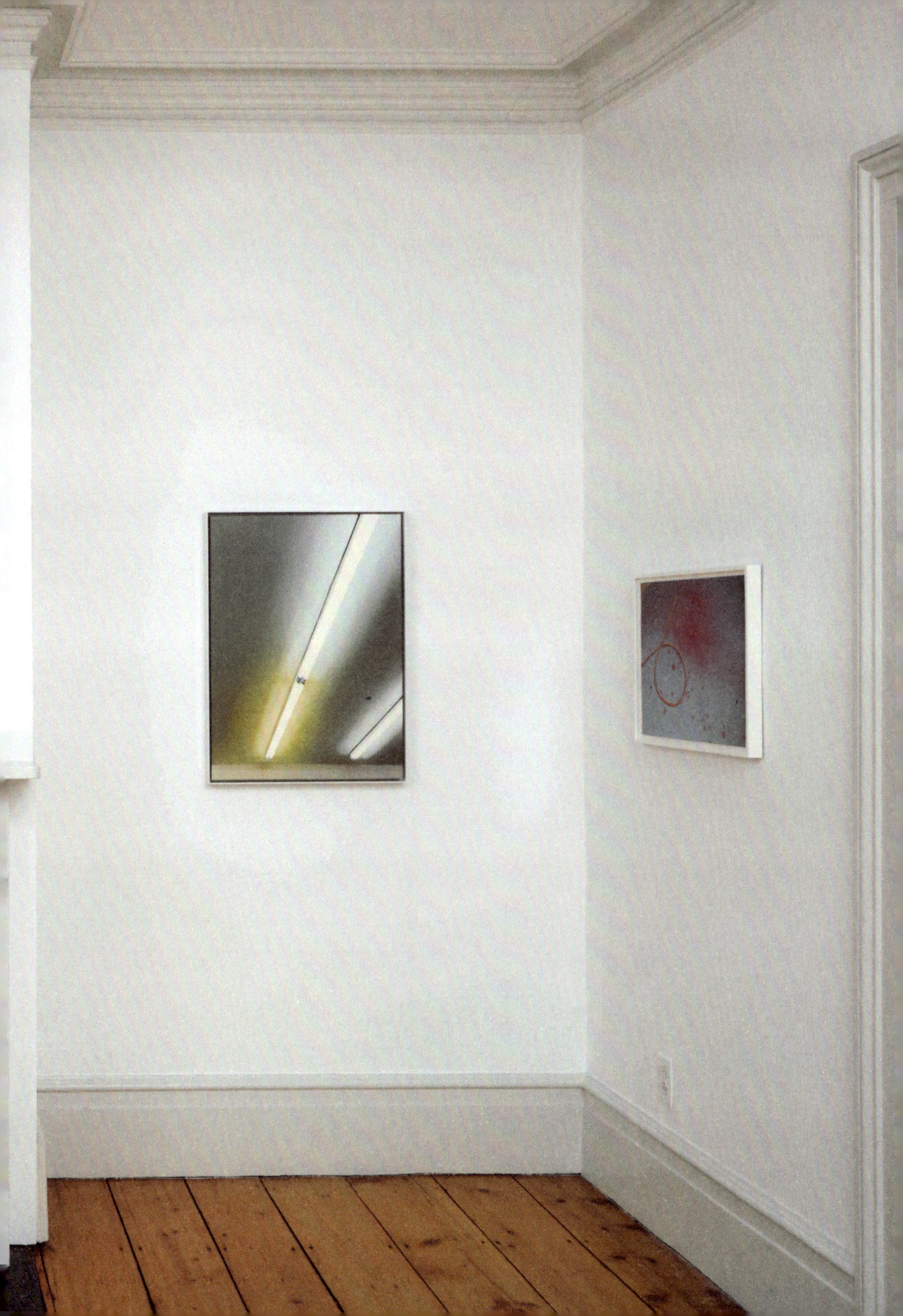

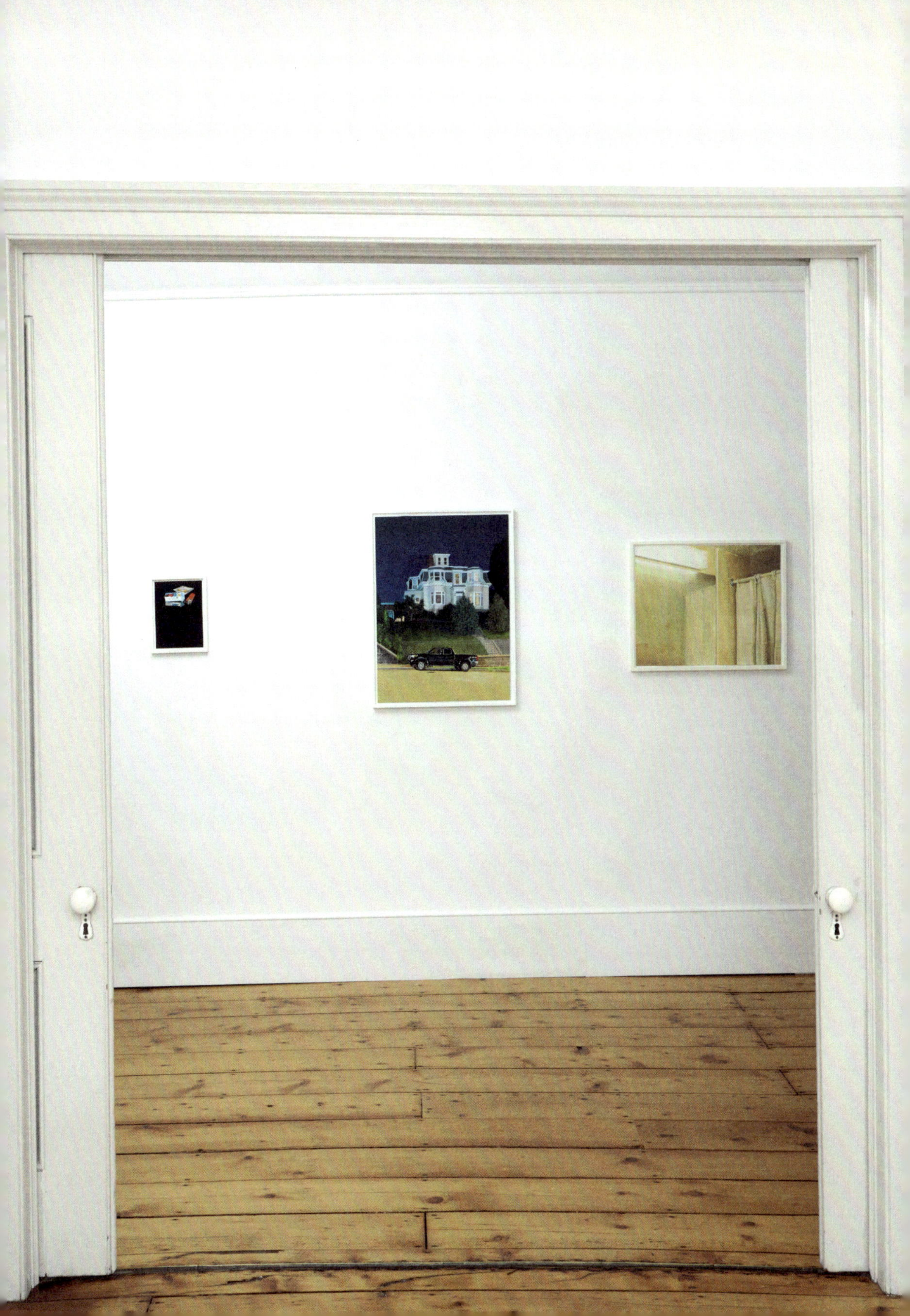

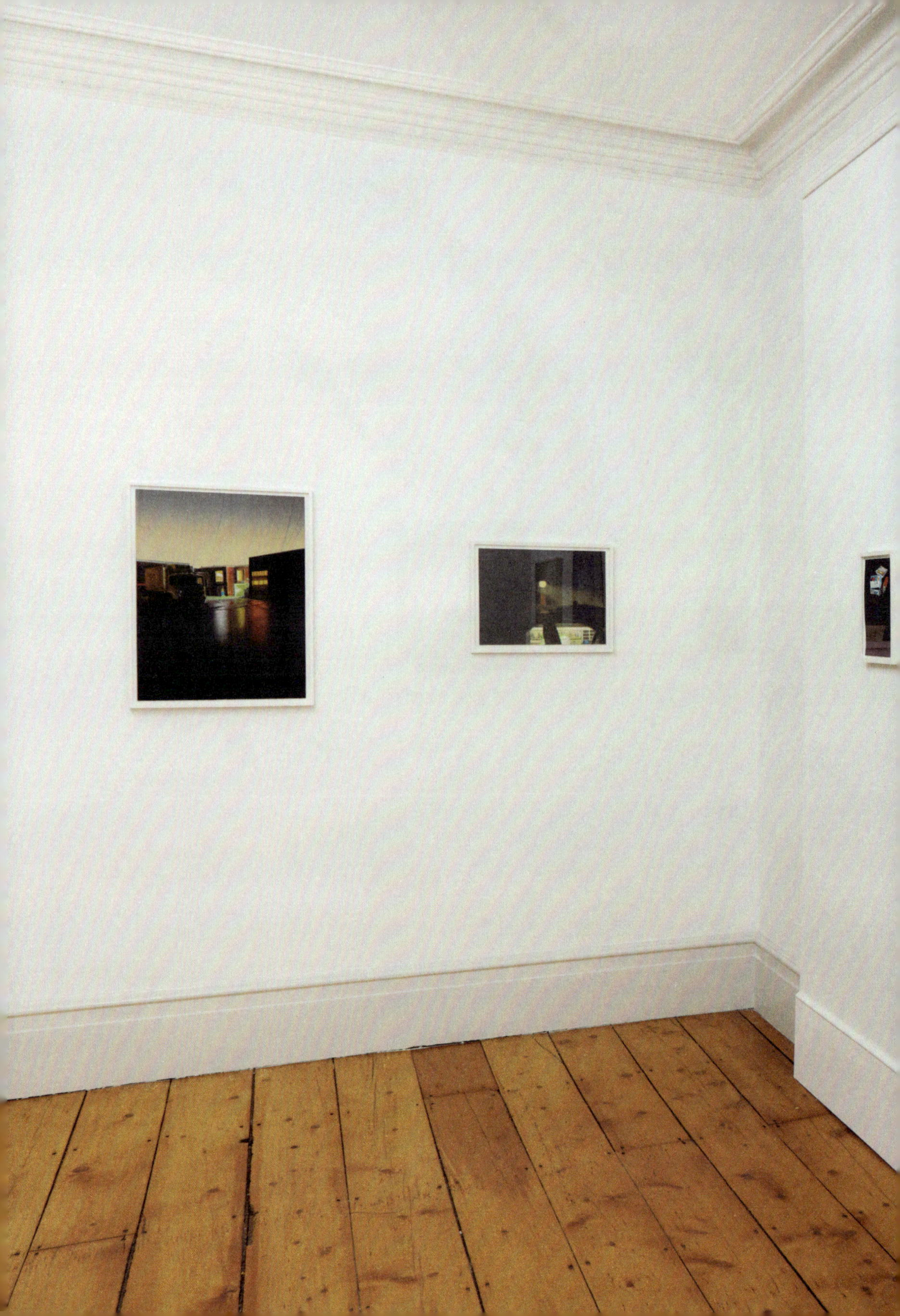

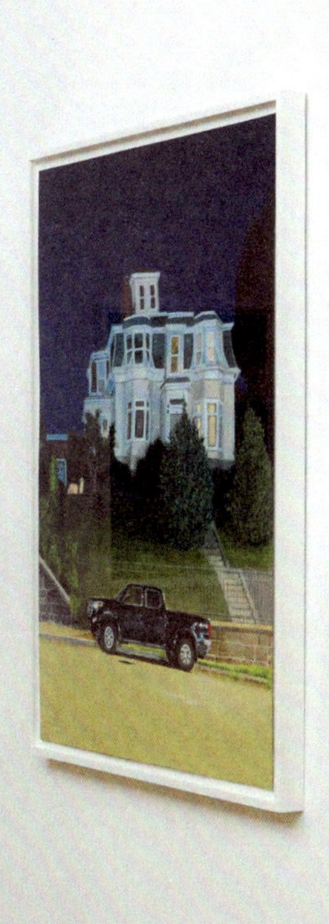
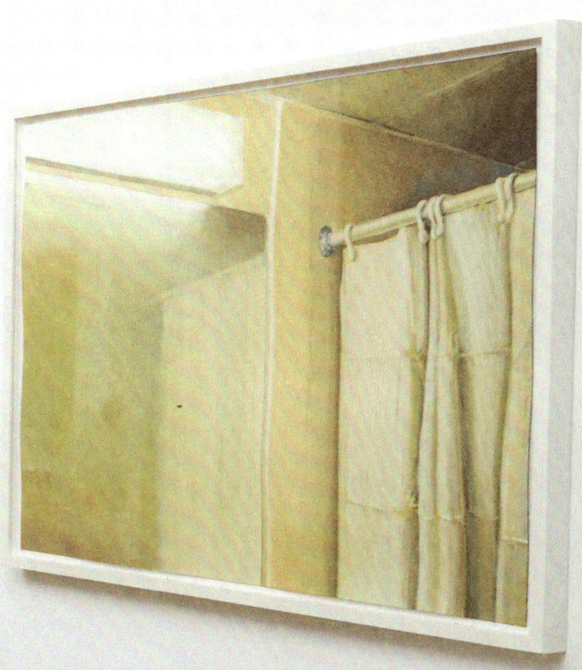

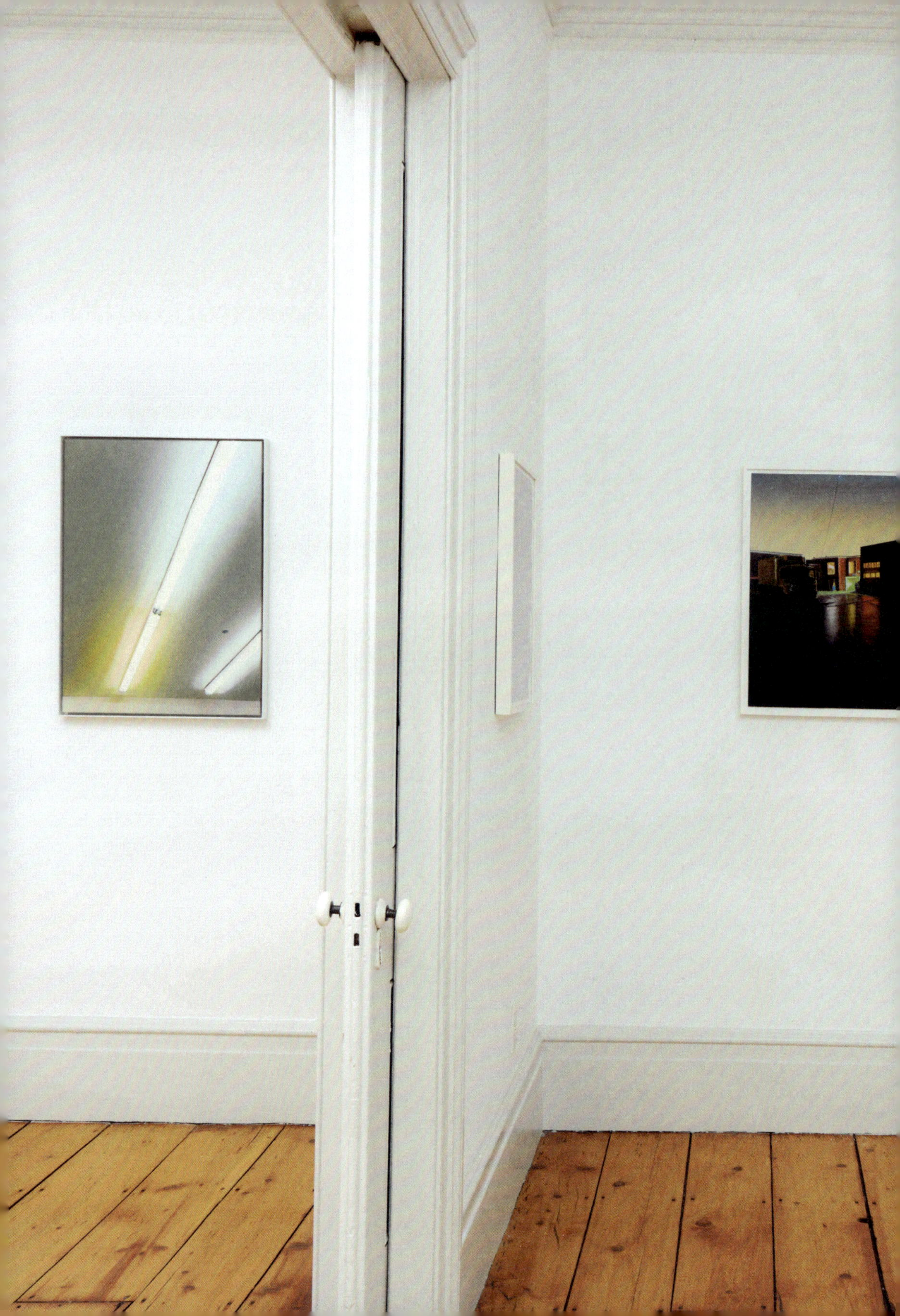

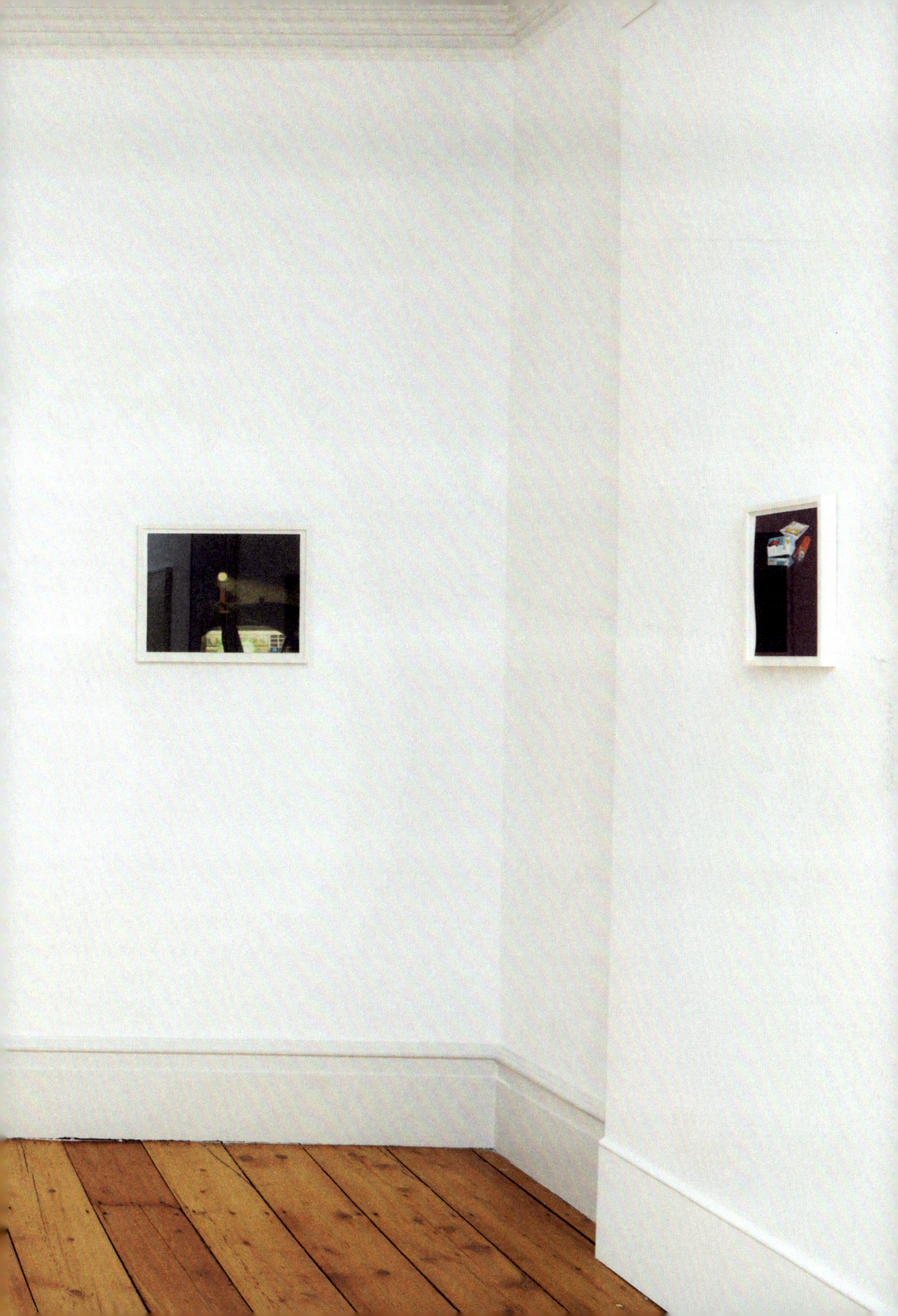

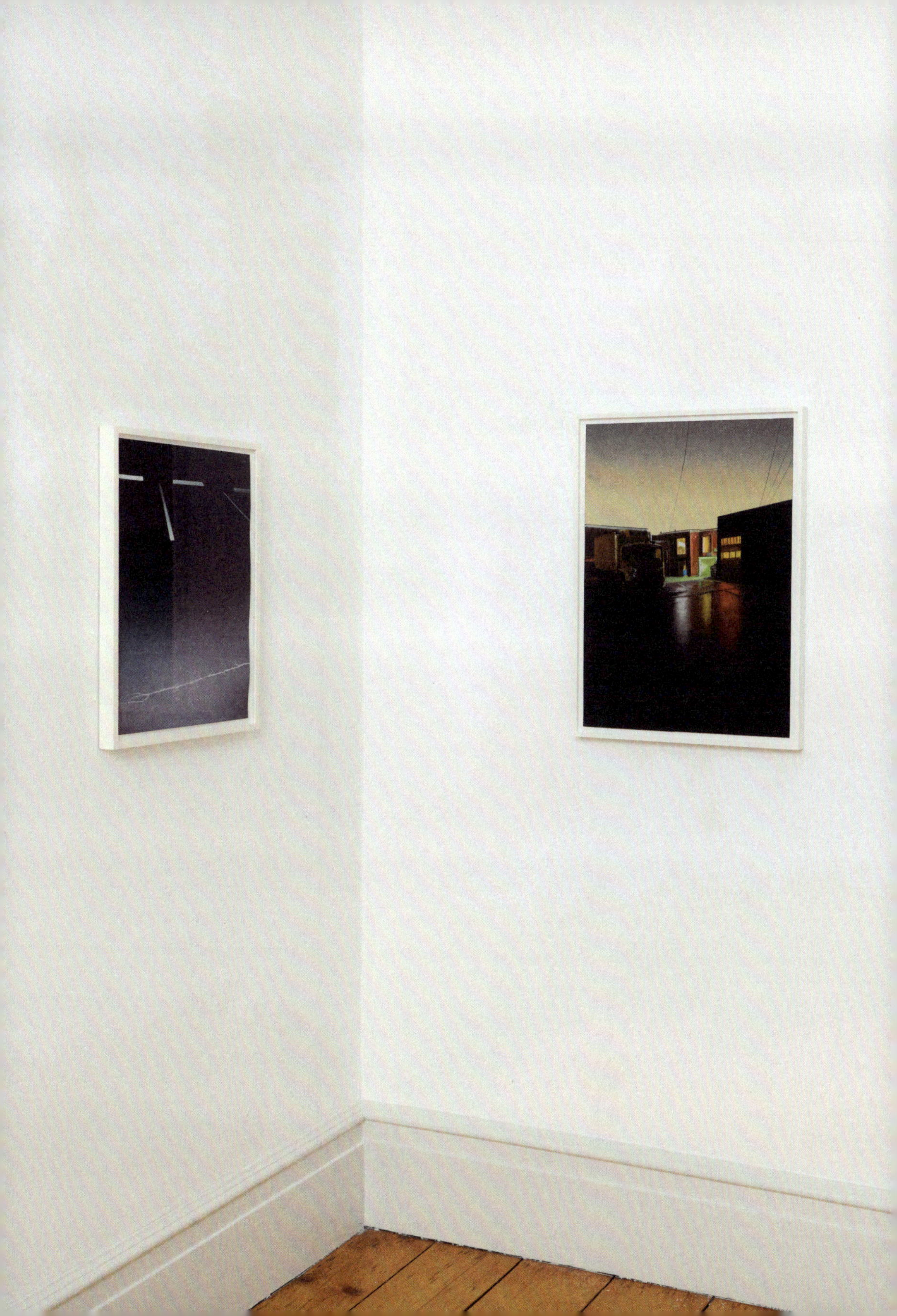

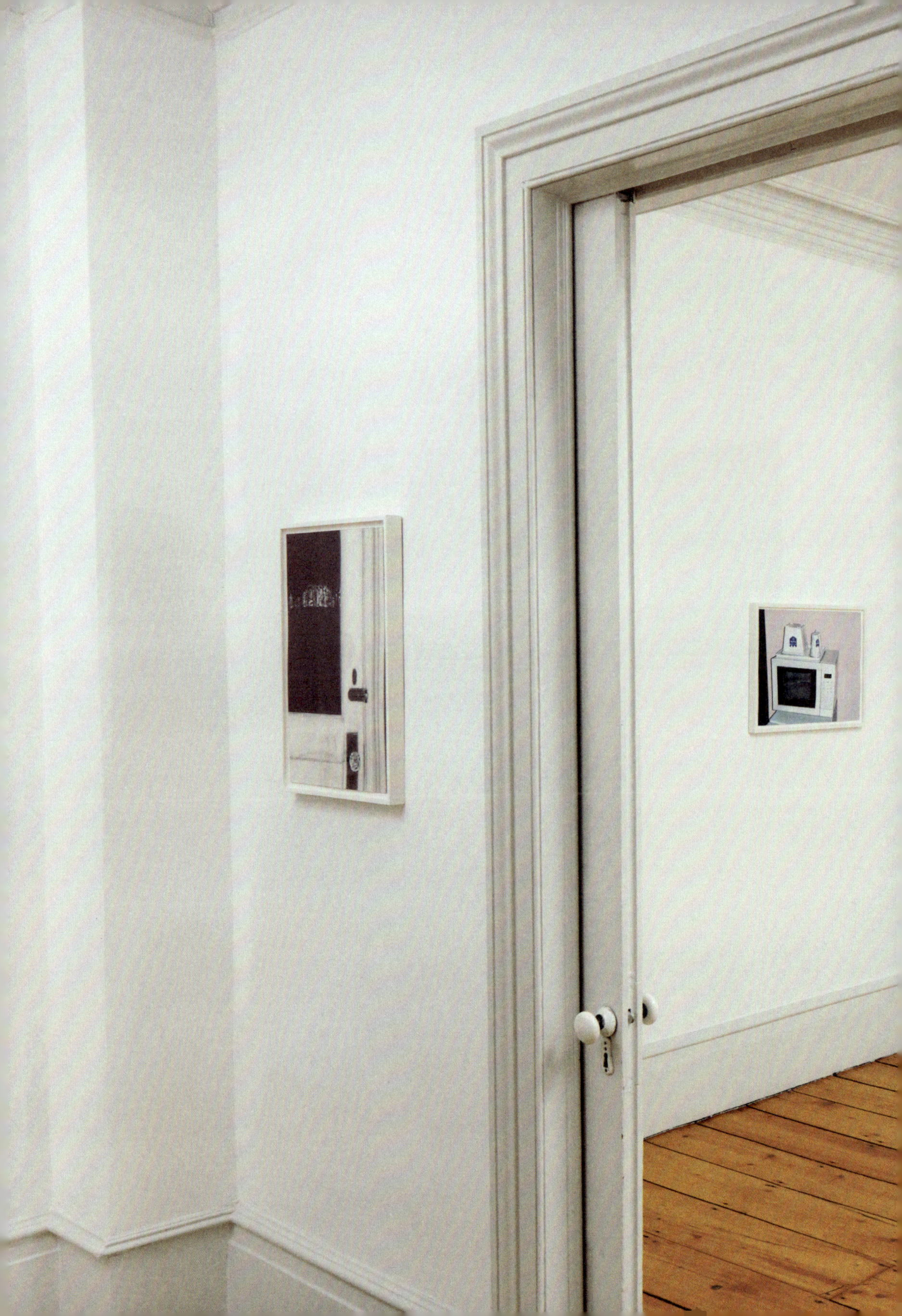

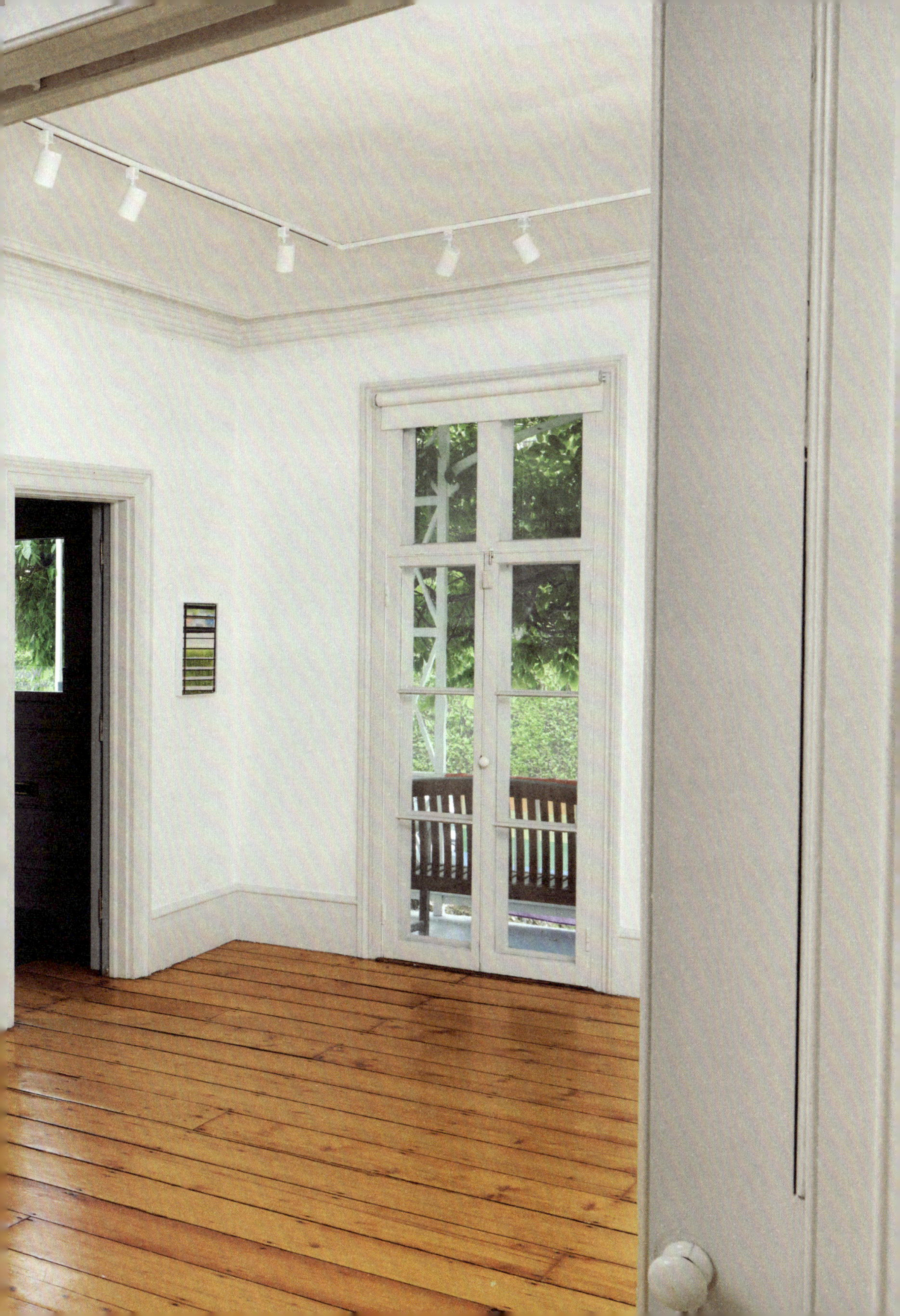

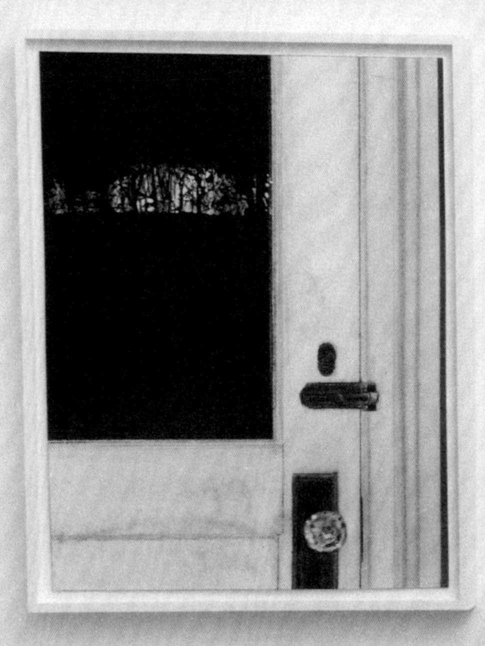

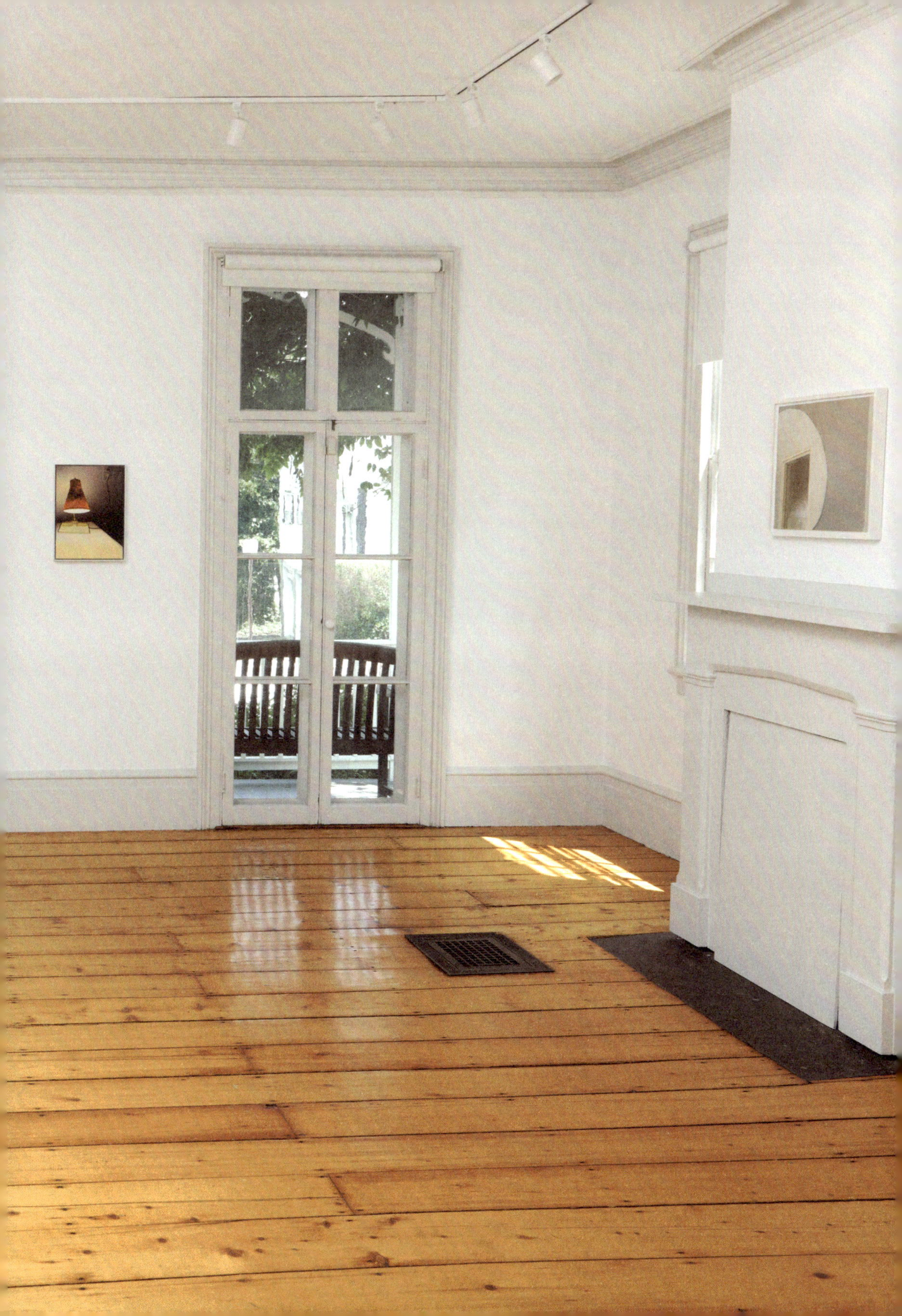

This book is published in conjunction with

Matinee: Dike Blair

Edward Hopper House Museum & Study Center
82 North Broadway
Nyack, New York
June 21–October 27, 2024

Matinee: Dike Blair © Edward Hopper House
Museum & Study Center

Edition of 750

Design and editorial: Karma Books, New York

Printed and bound in Belgium by die Keure

Photography credits: page 6: © The Museum of
Modern Art/Licensed by SCALA/Art Resource,
New York; pages 21, 22, 25, and 26: © Whitney
Museum of American Art/Licensed by Scala/Art
Resource, New York

ISBN 978-1-961883-18-5